Masonic Words and Phrases

Edited by
Michael R. Poll

Masonic Words and Phrases

A Cornerstone Book
Published by Cornerstone Book Publishers
Copyright © 2005 by Michael R. Poll

Cornerstone Book Publishers
Lafayette, LA

First Cornerstone Edition - 2005

www.cornerstonepublishers.com

Cover art, *The Proud Father*, is available at:
www.lostword.com

ISBN: 1-887560-11-4
ISBN 13: 978-1-887560-11-5

MADE IN THE USA

FORWARD

Freemasonry, when properly understood, is a life-long journey towards self-improvement. By means of presenting certain philosophical truths, the teachings of Freemasonry can offer an opportunity for living a more productive and rewarding life. There is, however, no final examination administered by grand lodges to determine when self-improvement takes place nor any attempt to determine ones level of self-improvement (if such a thing could be measured). Ours is a personal journey down the particular path we choose for ourselves. There is no rule that we must all walk the same path nor any yardstick used to measure our progress against another. The fact is that if one wishes to remain a member of a lodge, but make no attempt towards self-improvement, he may well remain a member of that lodge for life. If, however, one wishes to employ the teachings of Masonry with the goal of personal development, then a proper foundation is necessary.

The first steps to properly understanding the philosophical truths offered by Masonry require an understanding of the medium used to deliver these truths. In our case, this would mean an understanding of our symbols, words, usages and manner of presenting our instructions. By understanding these basic elements, our ways of teaching become clear and we can properly benefit from all that Masonry offers.

The goal of this work is to provide a handy and useful quick reference guide to many of the common words and phrases used in Masonry. While not designed to replace the education a new Mason receives from his instructor, this work can augment any study plan and provide valuable assistance to any Mason. This work is designed to be only one of many tools used by the dedicated student during his journey towards self-mastership.

Michael R. Poll
2005

Masonic Words and Phrases

A

Aaron

he was the brother of and "second in command" to Moses, and the first high priest under Mosaic dispensation; he was the founder of the "Aaronic" priesthood.

Aaron's Rod

the rod or staff carried by Aaron, brother of Moses, as a token of his office. The rod miraculously blossomed as evidence of his Divine choice as High Priest. It was afterwards preserved in the Ark of the Covenant.

Abhorrence of Evil

the quality required of all true Masons.

Abif

The "Abif" of Hiram Abif does not appear in the Bible. The word Abi or Abiw or Abiv is translated in the King James version both as "his father" and "my father" - using the word "father" as a term of respect and not as denoting a parent. Hiram, the widow's son of the tribe of Naphtali, was "my father" in the same sense that Abraham was "my father" to members of the tribes of Israel.

The thought that the two syllables are a surname is an error. The legend gains, not loses, in appeal when Abif becomes a title of honor. Just when and how it came into the Masonic terminology is still unknown; it does not appear in the Regis document (oldest of our Constitutions, dated approximately 1390) but does appear - only as one name among many - in the Dowland manuscript of 1550. Apparently the term was not in common use until after the King James Bible (1611) had become familiar in Masonic circles.

The story of Hiram Abif as told in the Masonic tale is not found in the Bible, nor is there any meaning in the word which can be construed as part of the story as Masons tell it, except that of veneration.

Abraham

in the Bible, the first patriarch and progenitor of the Hebrew people. He was the father of Isaac. Abraham was earlier known as Abram, the son of Terah of Ur. His name was changed to Abraham by God. He was noted for his faith, for piety, and for his loyalty to God.

Acacia

any of various often spiny trees or shrubs of the genus *Acacia* in the pea family, having alternate, bi-pinnately compound leaves or leaves represented by flattened leaf-stalks and heads or spikes of small flowers. Also, the Shittim tree. The wood of the Shittim tree is said to have been used for the furniture of the Temple of Solomon. In speculative Masonry, the term is often used as a symbol of the immortality of the soul.

Accepted

In Operative Masonry members were admitted through course of time, and when the Craft had begun to decay, gentlemen who had no intention of doing builders' work, but were interested in the Craft for social, or perhaps for antiquarian reasons, were "accepted" into membership; to distinguish these gentlemen Masons from the Operatives in the membership they were called the "Accepted." After 1717, when the whole Craft was revolutionized into a Fraternity, all members became non-Operatives, hence our use of the word in such phrases as "Free and Accepted Masons."

Accord

to make to conform or agree; bring into harmony. Required of all Masons in the philosophical sense in order to attain true Brotherhood.

Active Member

an active member is one who maintains his membership in a Masonic Lodge by the payment of his lodge dues and who takes part in the work and duties of the Craft. One who fails to do these things may remain a Mason at heart, but deprives himself of the benefits of active membership.

Adam

in the Bible, the first man and the husband of Eve. The name denotes that he was derived from the ground.

Adjournment

to suspend until a later stated time. The Worshipful Master is the most often the sole judge with reference to the adjournment of a Lodge, unless a time is fixed in the lodge bylaws.

Adhering Mason

There was a time in America (early 1800's) when the enemies of Freedom formed an anti-Masonic political party. The issues of the anti-Masons were brought before the people of the United States, and the anti-Masonic party was soundly defeated in a national election. The time, however, was still difficult for many Masons in different areas of the U.S. Those Masons who remained loyal to their lodges and grand lodges were called Adhering Masons. The "Adhering Mason" was then often scorned; now the term is one of honor.

Admonish

to reprove gently, but firmly. One of the most exacting duties in the ethics of Freemasonry is that a Mason should not publicize the faults of a Brother Mason, but shall whisper good, private counsel in his ear. An admonition must be given in the language of brotherly affection, the magic tongue of love, and with the persuasive attitude of "mercy unrestrained."

Adonai

used in Judaism as a spoken substitute for the ineffable name of God. While this proper name is not found in our English Bible, it occurs in several passages of the original Greek and Hebrew texts.

Adoration

the act of worship. A fundamental tenet of Freemasonry is that God is supreme, pre-eminent, and exalted above all creation, and that He alone is to be worshipped. Throughout all of the Degrees and in all of the ritual of Masonry, God is worshipped in adorations which are expressed in both silent and oral prayers.

Adversity

a state of hardship or affliction; misfortune. Freemasonry believes that adversity should be accepted as a test of character and met with courage and prayer. Also, a Mason should go to the aid of a Brother Mason in adversity.

Affiliate

to associate oneself as a subordinate, subsidiary, employee, or member. *Filius* is Latin for son, *filia* for daughter; the prefix "af" is a form of the Latin ad, meaning to add to. To be affiliated means therefore to be adopted into a family as a son or daughter, a meaning that beautifully covers a Mason's relation to their Lodge once they have affiliated with it.

Affirmation

something declared to be true; a positive statement or judgment. Affirmations instead of oaths are entirely inadmissible in Freemasonry.

Age, Lawful

this is the age when a man may apply to join a Masonic Lodge. In many jurisdictions, it is the age of twenty-one (21); in others, it is eighteen (18).

Ahiman Rezon

a book of Masonic law. The Antients' Grand Lodge of England published a Book of Constitutions in 1756, under the title "Ahiman Rezon, or a Help to a Brother." Eight editions were published in all before the Union of the two Grand Lodges in England in 1813. The title "Ahiman Rezon" was brought to America and used by several Grand Lodges; it is still the title of the books of law in Pennsylvania and South Carolina.

Aid of Deity

a fundamental principle of Freemasonry as illustrated in David's intercession for Solomon for the task of building the Temple.

Alarm

The Latin for weapons, or arms, was *arma*. Our "art" and "article" came from the same root, art meaning something originally made by the use of the arms, hands and fingers. The English "alarm" goes back directly to the Italian *alle arme*, and ultimately to the Latin ad *arma* so that "alarm" means "to arms, signifying that something has happened of possible danger. A knock at the Lodge door is so named because it calls for alertness, lest one unworthy be permitted to enter.

Allegiance

A Mason's first allegiance is to God, second to his family, then to his country and then to his Lodge.

Allegory

The Greeks called a place of public assembly agora; from this they built the word *agoreuein*, meaning speak, in the sense of addressing the public. When to this is added alias, meaning another, the compound gives us our "allegory," which is the speaking about one thing in the terms of something else. In Masonry we have the allegory of Solomon's Temple, of a journey, of the legend of a martyr builder, etc., in each case the acting and describing of one thing being intended to refer to some other thing. For example, the building of Solomon's Temple is described, not for the purpose of telling how that structure was erected, but to suggest how men may work together in brotherliness at a common task.

All-Seeing Eye

A perpetual and permanent symbol in the Lodge and work of Freemasonry, signifying the omnipresence and omniscience of God.

Almsgiving

helping the poor; a cornerstone of charity.

Altar

Alt, in Latin, referred to height, preserved in our "altitude;" this root appeared in *altare*, literally meaning a "high place." In primitive religion it was a common practice to make sacrifices, or conduct worship, on the top of a hill, or high platform, so that "altar" came to be applied to any stone, post, platform, or other elevation used for such purposes. The altar holds the central place in the Lodge room of Freemasons. Lying on the altar is the Holy bible, the principal Light of Masons, which is open during the work of the Lodge. Here, candidates voluntarily kneel and assume the obligations of the several Degrees.

Amen

used at the end of a prayer or a statement to express assent or approval. An expression by which one person confirms the word of another and expresses his wish for the success of that word. Following "Amen," Masons often employ the literal rendering of the word, "So mote it be."

Anchor

In those Degrees of Masonry where the ceremonies and instructions relate to life and death, man's journey over the sea of life is symbolized by Noah's Ark, and the hope of immortality and a safe landing in the haven of eternal security is symbolized by the anchor.

Anger

a strong feeling of displeasure or hostility. The tenets of Freemasonry teach its members to avoid and to subdue every element of ire and wrath, or enraged emotions and malicious emotions and sentiments.

Angle

the inclination of two lines meeting in a point. Angles are of three kinds-acute, obtuse, and right angles. The right angle, or the angle of 90 degrees, is the principal one recognized in Freemasonry.

Apprentice

one bound by legal agreement to work for another for a specific amount of time in return for instruction in a trade, art, or business. In Latin *apprehendre* meant to lay hold of a thing in the sense of learning to understand it, the origin of our "apprehend." This became contracted into *apprendre* and was applied to a young man beginning to learn a trade. The latter term came into circulation among European languages and, through the Operative Masons, gave us our "apprentice," that is, one who is beginning to learn Masonry. An "Entered Apprentice" is one whose name has been entered in the books of the Lodge having received the first degree of Masonry.

Apron

The Operative Masons wore a leather apron out of necessity; when the craft became speculative this garment, so long identified with building work, was retained as the badge of Masons. Hence, in the First Degree of Freemasonry, the initiate is presented with the pure white lambskin apron as a re-

minder of that purity of life and rectitude of conduct which is so essentially necessary to his gaining admission into the Celestial Lodge above where the Supreme Architect of the Universe resides forever. This apron becomes his permanent property as the "badge of a Freemason." As he advances in Masonry, he may receive other aprons of varying types, but never one that equals this first one in emblematic significance and Masonic value.

Arch, Holy Royal

Job compares Heaven to an arch supported by pillars. This is, of course, allegorical, even as is the name "Holy Royal Arch" degree in Masonry. The pillars which support the arch are emblematical of Wisdom and Strength; the former denoting the wisdom of the Supreme Architect, and the latter the stability of the universe.

Architecture

The five orders of architecture recognized in Freemasonry
are Doric, Ionic, Corinthian,
Tuscan and Composite. The
Doric order represents the West;
the Corinthian Column represents the South. The Gothic, or
pointed style of architecture, was
intimately connected with the
Middle Ages, over which Freemasonry maintained exclusive control.

Ark of the Covenant

The Ark of the Covenant was a chest originally constructed
according to specific instructions given to Moses by God, and
was the only article placed in the Holy of Holies in the Temple.
Within the Ark were placed the two tables or tablets of stone on
which the Ten Commandments were engraved, Aaron's baton
which had budded as a token of his divine appointment to the
office of High Priest, and a pot of manna.

Artificers

Tubal-cain was the first notable artificer mentioned in history. The best available of these master craftsmen were employed
in the building of the Temple.

Arts, Parts and Points

these terms are used in the mysteries of Masonry. Arts represents the knowledge or things made known; Parts, the degrees
into which Masonry is divided; and Points, the rules and usages
of Masonry.

Arts and Sciences

Freemasonry recognizes the seven principal arts and sciences as: Grammar, Rhetoric, Logic, Arithmetic, Geometry, Music and Astronomy.

Asher

in the Bible, a son of Jacob and the forebear of one of the tribes of Israel. In the tribal blessings promised to him, his tribe was to enjoy richness and royal dainties. Hence, entrusting the Masonic initiates with the mysteries of the Order is symbolized by the tribe of Asher.

Ashlar

a squared block of building stone. The Latin *assis* was a board or plank; in the diminutive form, *assula*, it meant a small board, like a shingle, or a chip. In early English this became *asheler* and was used to denote a stone in the rough as it came from the quarries. The Operative Masons called such a stone a "rough ashlar," and when it had been shaped and finished for its place in the wall they called it a "perfect ashlar." An Apprentice is a rough ashlar, because unfinished, whereas a Master Mason should be a perfect ashlar, because he has been shaped for his place in the organization of the Craft.

Ask, Seek, Knock

The applicant for membership in Freemasonry Asks for acceptance, Seeks for Light, and Knocks for initiation.

Atheism

the doctrine that there is no God. No atheist can become a

Mason in a lodge recognized by most jurisdictions. Every candidate must confess faith in God before crossing the threshold of the Lodge. This confession is an essential element in all the work of a Masonic Lodge.

Audi, Vide, Tace

these Latin words form the motto often found on Masonic medals and documents. They mean: *Hear, See, Be Silent.*

B

Backbiting

slandering a brother in his absence.

Badge of a Mason

see Apron.

Balloting

Balloting on the acceptance or rejection of a candidate is secret. Small round white balls and black cubes are used in the voting. White balls elect; black cubes reject. In casting the ballot, all lodge members are required to base their ballot on personal knowledge, information of the committee on investigation, and reputed character of

the candidate. Under no circumstances are members to allow themselves to be influenced by personal likes and dislikes of the candidate or by a spirit of prejudice or revenge.

Every member of the lodge is required to vote conscientiously for the good of the Order and in Brotherly consideration of the applicant.

Banishment

to drive away or expel. The practice of Freemasonry in banishing from its membership unworthy persons is fully sustained by Biblical authority and practice.

Barefoot

The removal of one or both shoes has been for many hundreds of years a token of reverence and a symbol of yielding one's self to the control and sovereignty of another.

Battery

In Masonry, a battery is normally specific raps of the gavels by the officers or claps of the hands by the members. A battery is a formal salute or Grand Honors; given in one form in public, in another in a tiled lodge.

Beauty

Operative Masonry has as its chief objective beauty and symmetry in architecture in building of King Solomon's Temple; speculative Masonry emphasizes the beauty of character and the virtues of true manhood.

Beehive

Among the ancients, the beehive was a symbol of an obedient
people and an emblem of system-
atized industry. Hence, Freemasonry has adopted the beehive as a
symbol on industry — a virtue
stressed in ritual and by lectures.

Benediction

an invocation of Divine blessing. A Lodge must never be
closed without a solemn prayer.

Benevolence

an inclination to perform kind, charitable acts. Freemasonry
is not to be classified as a benevolent institution; but the disposition and practice of benevolence is strongly stressed by the Fraternity.

Bible

masons accept this Book and
believe in it as the Law of God, as
the Great Light of Freemasonry. It
is an open Book on the altar during
all work of the Lodge, and certain
appropriate passages are used for
the different Degrees.

Bigotry

intolerance toward those of different creeds, races, nation-
alities or religious affiliations. Bigotry has no place in Freemasonry.

Blue

Blue is the accepted color of Freemasonry. As the color of the vault of Heaven, which embraces and covers the entire earth, it is to a Mason the symbol of universal friendship and benevolence. The name "Blue Lodge" or "Blue House" designates the Symbolic Lodge in which the first three degrees are conferred.

Boaz

in the Bible, the husband of Ruth. Signified by "strength," Boaz is the name of the left-hand pillar that stood on the porch of King Solomon's Temple, and adopted into speculative Masonry because of its symbolic meaning. It was broken to pieces by the Babylonians and carried to the city of Babylon.

Book of Constitutions
Guarded by the Tiler's Sword

reminds us that we should be ever watchful and guarded in our thoughts, words, and actions, particularly when before the enemies of Masonry; ever bearing in remembrance those truly Masonic virtues, silence and circumspection.

Book Of The Law

this is another name for the Holy Bible.

Brass

this metal was used extensively in the building of the Temple.

Brazen

made of brass

Brother

this word is one of the oldest, as it is one of the most beautiful, in any language. No one knows where or when it originated, but it is certain that it existed in the Sanskrit, in a form strikingly similar to that used by us. In Greek, it was *phrater*, in the Latin *frater*, whence our "fraternal" and "fraternalism." It has always meant men from the same parents, or men knit by very close blood ties. When associated with *initiation*, which has the general meaning of "being born into," one can see how appropriate is its use in Freemasonry. All of us have, through initiation in our "mother" Lodges, been born into a Masonry and therefore we are "brothers," and that which holds us together in one great family is the "Mystic Tie," the Masonic analogue of the blood tie among kinsmen.

Brotherly Love

Freemasonry recognizes the Divine requirement that godly men love their neighbors and that this love should be for all mankind. Emphasis is placed upon the privilege and duty of special love for members of the Fraternity. There are certain bonds and obligations in Freemasonry, which are fulfilled only in the spirit of true brotherhood.

Building of the Temple

Speculative Masonry has evolved indirectly from the organization of the workmen in the construction of Solomon's Temple and the union of operative masons who labored on that notable and Holy Building. Much of the subject of the ritual is traced directly back to the building of the Temple.

Burial

From time immemorial, Freemasons have given special attention to the interment of their dead, and the proper burial of a Brother Mason is regarded as a sacred and binding duty. Solemn, beautiful and profoundly meaningful burial rites and ceremonies are provided for deceased Brothers where such are requested by the Brother himself or by members of his family.

C

Cabletow

a compound word of Masonic coinage combining cable (a rope) and tow (a rope for pulling). Symbolically, it represents the covenant or first ties by which all Masons are bound.

Cable's Length

a maritime unit of length; about 100 fathoms or 600 feet. Can also mean the limit of a Mason's ability to do something.

Candidate

Among Romans it was the custom for a man seeking office to wear a shining white robe. Since the name for such a color was *candidus* (whence our "candid"), the office seeker came to be called candidate. In our ceremonies the custom is reversed: the candidate is clothed after his election instead of before.

Capital

the top part of a pillar or column.

Cardinal

of foremost importance; paramount. In Masonry we have "cardinal points" and "cardinal virtues." The Greeks had *kradan*, meaning, "swing on," and the Romans had *cardo*, meaning "hinge." The roots mean that on which a thing swings, or hinges, on which a thing depends or hangs, therefore anything that is of fundamental or pivotal, importance. A member of the Sacred College of the Roman Church is a Cardinal because of the importance of his office, which ranks next in dignity to that of the Pope. The cardinal points of the compass are those from which are determined all other points, north, east, south, west; the cardinal virtues are those which are fundamental to all other virtues.

Cardinal Points

East represents Wisdom; West, strength; South, beauty; North, darkness.

Cardinal Virtues

these are the principal virtues of which all others hinge. As set forth in the Entered Apprentice Degree, they are Temperance, Fortitude, Prudence and Justice.

Cedars of Lebanon

Among the finest and most perfect cedars ever known in history of the world were those of Lebanon. Through his alliance with Hiram, King of Tyre, Solomon secured cedars from these mountains for use in construction of the Temple.

Ceremony

The Latin *caerimonia* referred to a set of formal acts having a sacred, or revered, character. A ceremony differs from a merely formal act in that it has a religious significance; a formality becomes a ceremony only when it is made sacred. A "ceremony" may be individual, or may involve only two persons; a "rite" is more public, and necessarily involves many. An "observance" is public, as when the whole nation observes Memorial Day. A "Master of Ceremonies" is one who directs and regulates forms, rites and ceremonies.

Chambers

In the erection of King Solomon's Temple, a series of chambers were built on three sides of the Temple (north, south and west). This building against the wall of the Temple were three stories high (30 feet). These small chambers were used for Temple offices and for storage.

Charge

Among the most beautiful and forceful features of the work of Masonry are the solemn and exacting charges given to the candidate as he advances from one Degree to another.

Charity

The three great cardinal virtues are Faith, Hope and Love. Charity as an act of genuine, heart-felt love is so closely related that it is  sometimes employed in the place of Love, and is regarded as one of the three great cardinal virtues. The Greeks had a word, *charisma*, meaning a gift, and a number of words from the same root, variously suggesting rejoicing, gladness. The Latins had a similar word, *carus*, and meaning *dear*, possibly connected with am or, signifying love. From these roots came *grace*, meaning a free, unbought gift, as in the theological phrase, "the grace of God," and "charity." Strictly speaking, charity is an act done freely, and spontaneously out of friendship, not as a civic duty and grudgingly, as is sometimes the case in public charity. The Masonic use of the word is much nearer this original sense, for a Mason extends relief to a needy brother not as a duty, but out of caring.

Charter

In Latin *charta* was a paper, a card, a map; in Medieval Latin this became an official paper, as in the case of "Magna Charta." Our "chart" and "card" are derived from the same root. A Masonic charter is the written paper, or instrument, empowering a group of brethren to act as a Lodge.

Chasity

remaining pure in sexual relations.

Cipher

a reference book, printed by the Grand Lodge, containing much of the Masonic Ritual. It is encoded, and available to Master Masons with the permission of their Grand Lodge.

Circumambulation

to walk around something, especially as part of a ritual. In Masonic terminology this is the technical name of that ceremony in which the candidate walks around the Lodge. The word 4 is derived from the Latin prefix *cireum*, meaning "around," and *ainbulare*, meaning "walk," whence our ambulate, ambulatory, etc.; a circumambulation is therefore a walking around. In ancient religions and mysteries the worshippers walked around an altar; imitating the movements of the sun; this became known as circumambulation, and is the origin of our own ceremony.

Circumscribe

to draw a line around; encircle by the compasses; symbolic of the boundary line of Masonic conduct. To limit in range of activity definitely and clearly.

Citizenship

Perhaps no institution or organization has contributed more to good citizenship than Freemasonry. Democratic principles, good government, freedom of conscience and civic liberty have always been championed by Masons. Many of the world's great patriots and statesmen of all nations have been members of the Fraternity. Loyalty to one's government, faithfulness in all the duties of citizenship, and active support of public institutions are demanded throughout all the rituals of Freemasonry.

Clad

to cover as if with clothing.

Clandestine

In Anglo Saxon *helan* meant something hidden, or secret, a meaning preserved in "conceal;" "hell," the hidden place, is from the same word. Helan descended' from the Latin celare, hide; and on this was built the Latin clandestinus, secret, hidden, furtive. In English, clandestine, thus derived, came to mean a bad secret, one that must be indulged in furtively. A secret may be innocent; it is merely something done without the knowledge of others, and nothing is more common; but a clandestine act is one done in such a way as to elude observation. *Clandestine Masonry* has come to be regarded as a kind of irregular and unlawful secret society falsely claiming to be Masonic.

Clay Ground

the use of this term in Masonic work is based on the fact that a special clay found only in the Jordan Valley was used in casting the two great pillars, called Boaz and Jachin, which stood before the Great Porch of Solomon's Temple. This same clay was also used for casting ornaments and vessels used in the Temple.

Cleft

to split with or as if with a sharp instrument. An opening made by a crack or crevice; a hollow between two parts.

Clods of the Valley

this term is used in Masonic ritual in its Biblical meaning and signifies the sweetness of rest for the dead of the Lord.

Clothing

It has always been the custom among all peoples for designated officers, leaders, and people of rank to wear special regalia or a particular type of clothing which indicates a person's official position. Based on this custom and upon Biblical examples, and for reasons of dignity and beauty, Masons follow this practice.

In Masonic usage the meaning is much narrower and more technical; a Mason is clothed when he wears the apron and the emblem of his rank. The apron and gloves are also employed as symbols, though gloves have pretty much fallen into disuse in American Masonry.

Column

Three columns are employed to signify the supports of a Lodge; the columns of Wisdom, Strength and Beauty. The Greeks

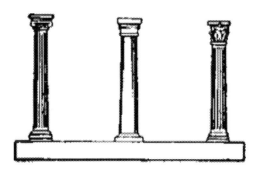

called the top or summit of anything kolophon; in Latin culmen had a similar meaning; from these origins come our culmination; excelsior, colophon, colonnade, colonel, and climax appears to he closely related to it. A "column" is a cylindrical, or slightly tapering, support; a "pillar" is a rectangular support. Either may stand free or be incorporated into the building fabric. The officers of a Lodge are figured as columns because they are the supports of the official fabric of the Lodge. The Great Pillars are symbolical representations of the two pillars, which stood on the Porch of King Solomon's Temple.

Common Gavel, The

The Common Gavel is an instrument used by operative Masons to break off the rough and superfluous parts of stones, the better to fit them for the builder's use. But we, as Free and Accepted Masons, are taught to make use of it for the more noble and glorious purpose of divesting our hearts and consciences of all the vices and superfluities of life; thereby fitting our minds as living stones for that spiritual building, that house not made with hands, eternal in the heavens.

Communication

A Masonic Lodge meeting is called a "communication" because it dates back to the earliest meaning of the word — the having of things in common, the fellowship of those engaged in a common purpose, governed by a common principle, and participation in common interests and activities.

Masonic communication is also understood to be the sharing of Masonic secrets with those entitled to such secrets. Masonic communication is *not* general, polite conversation with the profane or irregular Masons when no Masonic secrets are shared.

Compasses

The compasses are emblems of virtue, the true and holy measure of a Mason's life and conduct. This is the plural of compass, from the Latin *corn,* meaning "together," and *passus,* meaning a pass, step, way, or route. Contrivance, cunning, encompass, pass, pace derive from the same roots. A circle was once described as a compass because  all the steps in making it were "together," that is, of the same distance from the center; and the word, natural transition, became applied to the familiar two-legged instrument for drawing a circle. Some jurisdictions use the word in the singular, as in "square and compass," but the plural form "square and compasses" would appear to he preferable, especially since it immediately distinguishes the working tool from the mariner's compass, with which it might be otherwise confused by the uninformed.

Composite

one of the five orders of architecture, combining the Corinthian and Ionic styles

Consecration

Sacer was the Latin for something set aside as holy. By prefixing *con,* meaning "together," consecrare resulted, the general significance of which was that by adding to some holy object a formal ceremony the object was declared to be holy to the public, and must therefore be treated as such. The ceremony of consecrating a Lodge room is a way of giving notice to the public that it has been dedicated, or set aside, for Masonic purposes only.

Constituent Lodge

a Lodge chartered by, or under dispensation from, a Grand Lodge.

Constitution

Statuere meant that a thing was set, or placed, or established; when *con* was added *constituere* meant than an official ceremony had set, or fixed, or placed a thing. From the same source come statue, statute, institute, restitute, etc. A Lodge is "constituted" when it is formally and officially set up, and given its own permanent place in the Fraternity.

Contention

strife or struggle. Whenever and wherever men are grouped together for any purpose or a brotherhood is formed, differences of opinion will arise, conflicting interests will present themselves and the spirit of true brotherhood can be threatened. Among Freemasons, every effort must be put forth to prevent such circumstances from producing contention. Masons can agree to disagree.

Corinthian

one of the three classical (Greek) orders of architecture - the most ornamented of the three. Originated in the city of Corinth in Greece.

Cornerstone

this is usually the stone that lies at the corner of two walls of building in which certain historic documents are placed and on which historic inscriptions are engraved. In Masonic buildings, it is always placed at the northeast corner, and this position is preferred in buildings for which Masons perform the cornerstone-laying ceremony. Beautiful and meaningful symbolisms are associated with the laying of cornerstones as a dedication to the one living Great Architect of the Universe.

Covenant of Masons

A covenant is a contract or agreement between two or more parties on certain terms. In becoming a Mason, a man enters into a covenant with the Fraternity, agreeing to fulfill certain promises and perform certain duties. On the other hand, the Fraternity and its members bind themselves to certain ties of friendship, brotherliness, protection, support and benefits. The breaking of a covenant is subject to stated penalties.

Covering of a Lodge

The covering of a Lodge is no less than a clouded canopy, or starry-decked heaven, where all good Masons hope at last to arrive, by the aid of that theological ladder which Jacob in his vision saw ascending from earth to heaven; the three principal rounds of which are denominated Faith, Hope and Charity, and which admonish us to have faith in God, hope in immortality, and charity to all mankind. The greatest of these is charity; for our faith will be lost in sight; hope ends in fruition; but charity extends beyond the grave, through the boundless realms of eternity.

Cowan

the origin is unknown, but it may be early Scotch. A Masonic term which means intruder or one who accidentally enters where he is not wanted. This is not to be confused with the word eavesdropper or one who deliberately tries to overhear and see what is not meant for his eyes and ears.

Craft

In Anglo-Saxon, craft meant cunning, skill, power, dexterity, etc. The word became applied to trades and occupations calling for trained skill on the part of those practicing it. The distinction between such trades and those not requiring trained workmen, so rigidly maintained, was one of the hallmarks of the Middle Ages. Freemasonry is called a Craft, partly for historical reasons, partly because, unlike so many fraternities, it requires a training (given in the form of initiation ceremonies) of those seeking its membership.

Craftsmen

The term "craft" applies to persons collectively engaged in a trade or mechanical operation. It is used of operative Masons and the vast number of men employed in the building of the Temple are referred to as Craftsmen. In speculative Masonry, the entire Fraternity is spoken of as the Craft, whereas individual members are Craftsmen.

Cubit

an ancient unit of linear measure, originally equal to the length of the forearm from the tip of the middle finger to the elbow, or about 17 to 22 inches (43 to 56 centimeters). The sacred cubit is 36 inches; the profane cubit is 18 inches.

D

Darkness to Light

Physical darkness is symbolic of ignorance and of spiritual blindness. Applicants for the enlightenment of Freemasonry are, of course, in total ignorance of the rituals, teachings and symbols of the Order. They are, hence, required to enter the Lodge in complete darkness, symbolic of that ignorance. They are in search of Light, and this is given to them as they advance through the several Degrees of Masonry.

Dark

A lodge which closes for a time or permanently is said to be or have gone dark.

David

David was the youngest son of Jesse of Bethlehem who was chosen and anointed to become the successor of Saul as King of Israel while only a lad and shepherd of his father's flocks. He served King Saul as a musician, later as a military leader of some genius, bravery, and great heroism. However, he was bitterly persecuted by the King because of his jealousies. At the age of thirty, David was anointed King at Hebron and later established his throne at Jerusalem. He reigned forty years and was permitted by God to make extensive preparations for the building of the Temple which was later erected by his son and successor, Solomon. He was forbidden to build the Temple because he was a warrior while his son, Solomon, would be a man of peace.

Day

From the beginning, the period of twenty-four hours embracing one phase of light and one of darkness has been regarded as a day. Among the ancients, the day began at sunset and ended at sunset the next day instead of running from midnight to midnight.

Deacons

despite the fact that the bloom has been rubbed off by our slang use of it, this may be one of the most beautiful words in our language. In Greek, *diakonos* was a servant, a messenger, a waiting man. In the early Christian Church a deacon served at the Lord's Supper and administered alms to the poor; and the word still most frequently refers to such a church officer. It appears that the two Lodge offices of Senior and Junior Deacon were patterned on the church offices. Their duties comprehend general surveillance over the Lodge, the introduction of visitors, and to serve as proxy for the Worshipful Master in certain circumstances.

Death

The Masonic idea of death is accompanied with no gloom, because it is represented as physical sleep for an unknown period of time, from which there will be an awakening of the body and a resurrection of a spiritual body capable and fitted for eternal life. From beginning to end, the rituals of Freemasonry teach and symbolize the doctrine of man's immortality and repudiate every grain of the doctrine of *annihilation* at death. In Masonic philosophy, death is the symbol of initiation completed, in which the resurrection of the body will be its final consummation.

Decalogue

the Ten Commandments.

Dedication

The Latin *dedicatus* was a participial form of *dedicare*, the latter having the meaning of declare, devote, proclaim - the root from which "diction" comes. To dedicate a building means by public ceremony to declare it built for some certain purpose. Dedication and consecration are closely allied in meaning, but the latter is more religious in its purposes.

Degree

The Latin *gradus* from which are derived grade, gradual, graduation, etc., meant a step, or set of steps, particularly of a stair; when united with the prefix, *da*, meaning "down," it became degradus, and referred to steps, degrees, progress by marked stages. From this came our "degree," which is a step, or grade, in the progress of a candidate toward the consummation of his membership. Our habit of picturing the degrees as proceeding from lower to higher, like climbing a stair, is thus very close to the ancient and original meaning of the word.

Deputation

a group of words such as compute, repute, depute sprang from the Latin *putare*, which meant (among other things) to estimate, to think, to count among. From this came *deputatus*, to select, to appoint. The idea was that from a number of persons one was selected for a special duty, hence our word "deputy." A deputation is an instrument appointing some man or group of men to act for others officially. Our Deputy Grand Master is thus set apart to act in the place of the Grand Master on need, and a District Deputy Grand Master is so called because he is

appointed by the Grand Master to act as his personal representative in a District.

Demit

(also spelled "dimit.") as a verb this hails from the Latin
dimettere, to send away, to release, to let go; we have it in our
"dismiss." To demit from an organization is, using the official
form, to resign, to relinquish one's membership. It has this meaning in Masonry.

Destruction of the Temple

The Temple built by Solomon underwent many defamations
and was several times stripped of its golden adornments and
treasures, sometimes by foreign attacks and sometimes by Judean
kings for payments of tribute. These were judgments sent upon
the nation for apostasies. The final destruction of the Temple
was the burden of many prophecies and took place as predicted
by God under the onslaughts of the armies of Nebuchadnezzar
(586 B.C.).

Dew of Hermon

The dews of Mount Hermon, and of Palestine in general,
were sources of irrigation, fertilization and refreshment for veg-
etation and agricultural growth. The phrase is employed as a
symbolic expression of the bedewing influences of Divine Grace.

Discalceation

while this is not as familiar to Masons as the preceding
words, it should come into more popular use because it is the
technical name to describe an important element in the ceremony
of initiation. *Calceare* was the Latin for shoe, *calceatus* meant shod.
When united with the prefix *dis*, meaning apart, or asunder, our

discalceate was originated, the obvious meaning of which is the removal of one's shoes, as suggested in the familiar Bible passage, "Put off thy shoes from off thy feet, for the place whereon thou standest is holy ground." The ceremonial removal of the shoes is properly called the "rite of discalceation."

Dispensation

Pendere was the Latin word for a weight, the root from which came many English words, notably pendent, expend, spend, dispense, etc. With the prefix *dis*, explained in the preceding paragraph, dispendere meant to weigh out, to pay off, to expend. From this came dispensatus, meaning to manage, to regulate, to distribute. In our usage a dispensation is a written instrument by which authority is made over to a group of brethren to form a Lodge.

Distressed Worthy Brother

to go to the aid of a distressed worthy Brother is not only the duty of every Mason, but is solemnly enjoined by Holy Writ. Masons believe and practice the Bible's edict of "we are our Brother's keeper."

Divested

to deprive or take away from; to undress or remove clothing, ornaments or equipment.

Doors Shall Be Shut

The expression, "The doors shall be shut in the street when the sound of the grinding is low" refers to the decrepitude of old age.

Doric

one of the three classical (Greek) orders of architecture - the oldest and simplest of the three, originated in an area of ancient Greece known as Doris.

Dotage

An old man in his dotage is one who has suffered the loss of judgment and memory, and is in that state of intellectual decrepitude which makes him incapable of comprehending the lessons of Freemasonry. While it is not a very beautiful word, it is interesting. It first came into existence among the early English, Dutch, German, and Scandinavian peoples, generally in the form *dotten, dutten,* meaning to nod with drowsiness, to nap. Since it was old people who most frequently sat nodding in their chairs it became  associated with old age. "An old man in his dotage" is one who nods or prattles like a sleepy child, and whose faculties have begun to decay through old age. Old age is never a bar to Masonic membership unless it has reached this stage.

Due

proper; according to accepted standards or procedures

Dues

In Latin *debere* meant to owe something; it is preserved in our familiar, too familiar, "debt," in debit, indebted, debenture, duty, dues, etc. Related is the French *devoir,* often employed in English, meaning a piece of work one is under obligation to do. The same idea appears in "duty," which means that which is due, or that which is owed, in the moral sense. Dues represent one's fixed and regular indebtedness to his Lodge which he placed himself under obligation to pay when he signed the by-laws.

Dust to Dust (or Dust To Earth)

Man's body was made from the earth and must return to dust in one form or another. The use of this phrase points to the mortality and frailty of the physical being and to the need of recognizing the immortality of the spirit of man.

E

Eavesdropper

Early European peoples used a word in various forms - *evese*, *obasa*, *opa*, etc., - which meant the rim, or edge, of something, like the edge of a field; it came in time to be applied wholly to the gutter which runs along the edge of a roof. (Our "over" comes from this root.) "Dropper" had an origin among the same languages, and meant that which drips, or dribbles, like water dropping from a thawing icicle. Eavesdrop, therefore, was the water which dripped from the eaves. If a man set himself to listen through a window or keyhole to what was going on in a house he had to stand so close that the eavesdropping would fall upon him, for which reason all prying persons, seeking by secret means what they have no business to know, came to be called eaves-droppers.

Edict

a decree or proclamation issued by an authority and having the force of law. The root of this word is the Latin *dicere*, speak; united with the prefix *e*, meaning out, to come forth, it produced *edicere*, meaning to proclaim, to speak out with authority. It came in time to be applied to the legal pronouncements of a sovereign or ruler speaking in his own name and out of his own authority. When a Grand Master issues a certain official proclamation in his own name and out of the authority vested in his office, it is an edict.

Edifice

a building, especially one of imposing appearance or size.

Emblem

This beautiful and significant word, so familiar to Masons, has historical affiliations with the original idea embodied in "mosaic work," on which something is said below. Emblem is derived from the Greek prefix *en*, meaning in, united with *ballein*, meaning cast, put. The word became applied to raised decorations on pottery, to inlay work, tessellated and mosaic work; and since such designs were nearly always formal and symbolical in character, emblem came to mean an idea expressed by a picture or design. As Bacon put it, an emblem represents an intellectual conception in a sensible image. It belongs to that family of words of which type, symbol, figure, allegory, and metaphor are familiar members.

Emblem of Innocence

Throughout the Holy Scriptures, the lamb is used as an emblem of innocence, and the white leather lambskin apron is regarded as an emblem of purity after which Masons ever strive for in life.

Engrave

to cut figures or letters into wood, metal or other material

Ephraimites

members of one of the twelve tribes of Israel, descended from Ephraim, one of the sons of Jacob

Esoteric

this word is the opposite of exoteric. The root of it is the Greek *eso*, within. It means that which is secret, in the inner circle. Exoteric is that which is outside. In Masonry the "esoteric work" is that part of the Ritual, which it is illegal to publish, while the exoteric is that part which, is published in the Monitor.

Etch

to produce as a pattern on a hard service by eating into the material's surface as with acid or any means of shallow scratches

Equivocation

the use of equivocal language, e.g., words capable of two interpretations, cryptic, evasive, ambiguous - to avoid committing oneself to what one says; uncertainty; uncertain or questioning disposition or mind

Eternal Life

The immortality of the soul is a fundamental dogma of Freemasonry. Hence, the faith and belief in eternal life beyond the grave. The doctrine of a future resurrection of the body is also a tenet of Freemasonry.

Evergreen

having foliage that persists and remains green throughout the year. In Masonry, the evergreen is used as a symbol of the immortality of the soul.

F

Faithful Servant

The faithful servant is one who is diligent in his stewardship, dutiful to his master and loyal in the face of temptation and trial.

Fatherhood of God

Masonry believes that man is the offspring of God by creation, that God made mankind all of one blood and that God is, by virtue of His creation of man and of His goodness to man, man's Father.

Fellow

In Anglo Saxon, *lagu* (from which we have "law") meant that which was permanently ordered, fixed, set; *fe* meant property; *fela* suggested properties set together, in other words, a partnership. From this we have "fellow," a companion, mate, partner, an equal, a peer. A man became a "fellow" in a Medieval guild or corporation when admitted a member on the same terms as all others, sharing equally in the duties, rights, and privileges. In Operative Masonry, in order to be a fellow a man had to be a Master Mason, in the sense of having passed through his apprenticeship, so that Masters were fellows and fellows were

Masters. Prior to about 1740 "Fellow of the Craft" and "Master Mason" referred to the same grade or degree, but at about that year a new division in ranking was made, and "Fellow Craft" was the name given to the Second Degree in the new system, "Master Mason" to the Third.

Fiat

an authoritative decree, sanction or order; a command or act of will that creates something without, or as if without, further effort; an arbitrary decree or order.

Fiat Lux

Latin for: *Let There be light*

Flight to Joppa

The story of Jonah's flight to Joppa in his effort to escape a Divinely-entrusted responsibility and service for God is strikingly used in Masonic ritual.

Foreign Country

This expression, which is employed of the travels of Master Masons of the operative class following the completion of the Temple in search of labor and for wages, is correctly understood by few who hear it. In its symbolic meaning, it does not refer to the activities of those who have completed the Master Degree. Hence, Heaven is the "foreign country" into which Master Masons travel, where the True Word, not given in this life, is to be received, and where the Master Mason is to receive his wages.

Form

We speak of the "form of the Lodge," "due form," etc. The

word is derived from the Latin *forma*, which meant the shape, or figure, or frame of anything; also it was used of a bench, or seat, whence the old custom of calling school benches "forms." It is the root of formal, formation, informal, and scores of other English words equally familiar. The "form of the Lodge" is its symbolical shape; a ceremony is in "due form" if it has the officially required character or framework of words and actions.

Fortitude

The key to the meaning of this magnificent word lies in its derivation from the Latin *fords*, meaning strong, powerful, used in the Middle Ages of a stronghold, or fort. Force, enforce, fortify, fortification, forceful, are from the same root. A man of fortitude has a character built strong like a fort, which can be neither taken by bribe nor over-thrown by assault, however strong may be the enemy, or however great may be the suffering or deprivation within. One is reminded of Luther's great hymn, "A mighty fortress is our God." The importance and essential value of this virtue of true manhood for Masons is enforced by the use of the story of unfaltering courage and faith of the three Hebrew children in the fiery furnace and by Daniel's bravery in the lion's den.

Foundation

The deeply laid and solid foundation of the Temple strikingly symbolizes the necessity for a good foundation in the building of character and in life's vocations.

Forty-Seventh Problem of Euclid

The forty-seventh problem of Euclid's first book, which has been adopted as a symbol in the Master's Degree, is thus enunciated: "In any right-angled triangle, the square which is described upon the side subtending the right angle is equal to the squares described upon the sides which contain the right angle." Thus, in a triangle whose perpendicular is 3 feet, the square of which is 9, and whose base is 4 feet, the wquare of which is 16, the hypotenuse, or subtending side, will be 5 feet, the square of which will be 25, which is the sum of 9 and 16. This interesting problem, on account of its great utility in making calculations and drawing plans for buildings, is sometimes called the "Carpenter's Theorum."

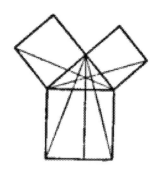

This was an invention of our ancient friend and brother, the great Pythagoras, who, in his travels through Asia, Africa, and Europe, was initiated into several orders of Priesthood, and raised to the sublime degree of Master Mason. This wise philosopher enriched his mind abundantly in a general knowledge of things and more especially in Geometry, or Masonry. On this subject he drew out many problems and theorems; and among the most distinguished, he erected this, which, in the joy of his heart, he call Eureka, in the Grecian language signifying, I have found it; and upon the discovery of which he is said to have sacrificed a hecatomb. It teaches Masons to be general lovers of the arts and sciences.

Fraternal Intercourse

activities that promote fraternalism in constituent Lodges. This is normally held to be the exchange of words, signs and grips that are reserved for known Masons.

Fraternity

This the most prized, perhaps, of all words in Masonry, harks back to the Latin *frater*, which is so closely allied to "brother," as already noted in the section on that word. It gives us *fra, frater, fraternize*, and many other terms of the same import. A fraternity is a society in which the members strive to live in a brotherly concord patterned on the family relations of blood brothers, where they are worthy of the tie. To be fraternal means to treat another man as if he were a brother in the most literal sense.

Free

The origin of the use of the term "free" in speculative Masonry is in the fact that the operative Masons who worked on King Solomon's Temple were exempted from imposts, duties and taxes as were their descendants. They were, therefore, declared to be "free."

G

"G"

The letter "G" is one of the most sacred symbols in Freemasonry. It has a double meaning, representing, first, the Supreme Deity as the Great Architect of the Universe and the one true and living God of all Masons; and, secondly, the pre-eminence of the science of geometry in the rituals of Freemasonry. In this twofold symbolism, the letter "G" represents to the Mason unity of Heaven with the earth, of the Divine Being with the human, of the temporal with the eternal, and of the finite with the infinite.

Gage

Gage (also spelled "gauge") has an uncertain ancestry. Early French and English peoples had *gauger, gagen,* etc., which referred to the measuring of wine casks; some believe our "gallon" and "gill" to have been thus derived. Its meaning became enlarged to include any kind of measuring, literally or figuratively. The instrument used to do the measuring came to be called "the gage." Among Operative Masons it was used to measure a stone for cutting to the required "twenty-four-inch gage" is such a measuring rod or stick marked off into twenty-four inches.

Gates of the Temple

The Temple of Solomon had only one entrance or portal, but the walls of the enclosure had a gate at each points of the compass. Freemasonry makes special symbolic use of three of these gates, the one on the east, the one on the west, and the one on the south. These gates are symbols of the progress of the sun, rising in the east, reaching its zenith in the south, and setting in the west. They also symbolize birth, life, and death as well as youth, manhood and old age.

Geometry

It is unfortunate that for most schoolroom drudgery has robbed this beautiful word of its poetry. The Greek *geo* (in compounds) was earth, land; *metron* was measure. The original geometer was a landmeasurer, a surveyor, but his methods be-

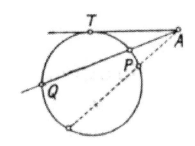

came broadened and applied to many other kinds of problems, so that at last his craft became a portion of the art of mathematics. Geometry, that branch of mathematics which deals with figures in space, is associated in every Mason's mind with the immortal Euclid, who figures 50 prominently in all the ancient Masonic manuscripts. It achieved its great place in Freemasonry because of its constant and prime importance in the builders' art. Symbolically speaking geometry (to it the Letter G originally referred), consists of all those fixed principles and laws of morality and of thought to which a right character and a true mind adjust themselves.

Good Standing, In

when dues are current and one is an Active Member of the lodge or when one is defined as such by the lodge or Grand Lodge laws

Grammar

The Greeks had *graphein*, to write, or draw (from this we have graphic, engrave, etc.) ; gramma was that which was written or drawn. Grammar now refers only to the skeletonal framework of language, its parts of speech and their combinations, but formerly it included all forms of learning based on language, such as rhetoric and what is now taught in the schools as English; by the time our Monitors were written, however, grammar and rhetoric had become differentiated. In interpreting the Second Degree this wide meaning of "grammar" must be kept in mind.

Grand

Grandis in the Latin meant great, large, awesome, especially in the sense of imposing; it was afterwards applied to the aged, the ripe in experience, an application easy enough to understand when one recalls the reverence paid by the Romans to seniority, long experience, etc. this latter meaning appears in our grandfather, grandmother, grandsire, etc. In English the word developed in two directions, one toward that which is great, large, awe-in-spiring, as in "grandeur," the other toward dignity, exalted power. Our own use of the term in "Grand" Lodge, "Grand" East, "Grand" Master, harks back to the latter of the two usages. The head of the Craft is called "Grand"' Master because he is its most exalted official.

Grasshopper Shall Be A Burden

symbolic of the weakness accompanying old age.

Great Porch

this was the name give to the vestibule at the entrance into the Temple of Solomon.

Great and Sacred Name

Any name that is used as a title of Deity is held sacred by Freemasons, and all names of our God are to be uttered with profound reverence and never thoughtlessly or blasphemously.

Great White Throne

this term refers to the pure and glorious throne of God. Before it, every knee must bow to the Glory of the Father.

Grip

Grip, grope, grab, grasp, gripe came the same roots. The Anglo Saxon *gripe* meant to clutch, to lay hold of, to seize, to grasp strongly. A grip means

to clasp another's hand firmly; it differs from a mere handclasp, which may be a meaningless formality, in that it is done earnestly, and for a purpose—for what purpose in our fraternal system every Mason knows. A grip should be given as if one meant it; half of its meaning lies in the way it is done.

Ground Floor of the Lodge

Mount Moriah, the site on which Solomon's Temple was erected, is symbolically referred to as the "ground floor of the Lodge."

Guttural

from the Latin *guttur*, the throat, or having to do with, or involving the throat

H

Harodim

the title given to the overseers and princes appointed by Solomon to supervise the workmen preparing the material and in the building of the Temple.

Hecatomb

a sacrifice to the ancient Greek and Roman gods consisting originally of 100 oxen or cattle.

Healing

Healing is a process used in some jurisdictions to accept a Mason from an irregular lodge into a regular lodge. The process may be but an administrative procedure or may be one of retaking some or all of the craft degrees or obligations.

Heaven

A distinctive tenet of Freemasonry is that there is a Heaven of bliss beyond the grave. The symbolic meaning of the "foreign country" in which the Master Mason seeks wages is Heaven, the higher state of man's existence after death and following the Resurrection.

Hele, Hale

to hide or conceal; to cover; to keep out of view.

Heredom

The most plausible understanding of "Heredom" was given in 1858, by a writer in the London Freemasons Magazine. He traces it to the two Greek words, *repass hieros*, meaning holy, and *biros domos*, meaning house. It would thus refer to Freemasonry as symbolically the Holy House or Temple. In this way the title of Rose Croix of Heredom would signify the Rosy Cross of the Holy House of Freemasonry. This derivation is now very generally recognized as the true one.

High Twelve

The Latin *nonus* referred to the ninth hour of the day, that is, nine hours after sunrise. In the Medieval church it referred to the middle hour between midday and sunset, that is, about three o'clock P.M. In the course of time it came to refer to any part of the middle of the day, and finally to twelve o'clock. The origin of our "High Twelve" is uncertain, but it is probable that it goes back to a time before "noon" was generally used for twelve o'clock; the "high" doubtless refers to the sun, which at that time was at its highest point in the sky.

Hills and Valleys

In ancient times, and even today, high elevations suggest the worship of God. The hilltop or mountaintop is a symbol of "Holiness unto the Lord."

Hiram

The gavel, when wielded by the Master of the Lodge, is sometimes called the Hiram, because as the workmen at the Temple were controlled and directed by Hiram, the chief builder, so the Master keeps order in the Lodge by proper use of the gavel.

Hiram Abif

see: *Abif*

Homage

special honor or respect shown or expressed publicly.

Hoodwink

"Hood" goes back to old German and Anglo Saxon, in which it referred to head covering, as in hat, hood, helmet, etc.; "wink," in the same languages, meant to close the eyes, "wench," "wince," etc., being similarly derived. A hoodwink was therefore a headdress designed to cover the eyes. The popular use of the word is believed to go back to the old sport of falconry, once so popular, in which the falcon had a hood over its eyes until ready to strike at its prey.

Holiness

Throughout Masonic ritual, the absolute and superlative Holiness of God is recognized, and every representation of the

Deity in symbols, attitudes and words must be in the most reverent manner.

Holy of Holies

The ancient Tabernacle erected by Moses at Mount Sinai was divided into two compartments or rooms. At the west end was the Most Holy Place constructed of a perfect cube fifteen feet in all dimensions. It was separated from the other room, the Holy Place, by curtains. The only article of furniture in the Holy of Holies was the Ark of the Covenant which contained the Book of Law, the stone tablets on which God had written the Ten Commandments, a pot of manna and Aaron's rod that budded. The Most Holy Place was entered only by a high priest once each year on the Great Day of Atonement. Like the Tabernacle, King Solomon's Temple was divided into two compartments. The Most Holy Place was a perfect cube forty feet in all its dimensions. All the walls were overlaid with fine gold as was the floor.

Holy Place

One of the two compartments of the Tabernacle of Moses was the Holy Place or Sanctuary at the east end of the Tabernacle. The furniture of the Holy Place consisted of the great Candlestick, the table for shewbread and the altar of incense with its censer and snuffers. In King Solomon's Temple, the Holy Place, sometimes referred to as the Greater House, followed the pattern of the Tabernacle, but was much larger. Instead of one candlestick, there were ten: five on the right side and five on the left, all made of pure gold. The Altar of Incense occupied the west end of the Sanctuary and was also made of pure gold, as was it censer.

Hour Glass, The

is an emblem of human life. "Behold how swiftly the sands run, and how rapidly our lives are drawing to a close!"

House

This term is used to mean any of the various Masonic bodies. A "Blue House" would be a craft lodge.

House Not Made With Hands

This expression comprehends the eternal dwelling place of God and the resurrected and glorified body of the redeemed in the life beyond.

Human Senses

There is here the recognition of the truth that all the natural faculties and endowments of man are the products of the creative energy of God and are loving gifts from Him.

I

I Am That I Am

This is the English translation of the most distinctive and significant title of Jehovah God given to Moses at the burning bush. In its original Hebrew form, it was regarded with such sacredness by the Israelites that it was never spoken above a whisper. It signifies the "self-existent, independent, unsearchable One."

Immemorial

Reaching beyond the limits of memory, tradition, or recorded history.

Immortality

Much of the ritual in Freemasonry assumes the doctrine of man's immortality, and in many specific instances, professions of this fundamental tenet are uttered.

Impart

to give; to communicate knowledge of something; to make known; tell; relate

Indite

to write down; to put down in writing

Indwelling of God

That God deigns to dwell among his people and with the hearts of the pure and the good is a fundamental truth to Masons.

Ineffable Name

It is generally agreed among the Believers that the correct pronunciation of the most sacred name of God has been lost, and to this traditional fact Masons assent. In it believed, however, that the mysteries of this Ineffable Name is held by the Messiah until the Day of Resurrection.

Initiation

The Latin *initium* means beginning, as in our initial"; *initiatus*, the participle from the verb *initiare*, referred to any act incident to the beginning or introduction of a thing. The word came widely into use in mysteries and sacred rites, whence it has come into our Masonic nomenclature. Back of it, as used by us, is the picture of birth, so that the Masonic initiation means that a candidate has been born into the Masonic life, making the same kind of symbolic beginning therein that a babe makes when born into the world.

A Masonic initiation is a personal, meaningful experience where there has been a desire to initiate, a desire to be initiated and the proper, solemn setting for the initiation.

Injunction

an order or requirement placed upon someone by a superior

Inner Door

Just as the mysteries of God's truth are available to those who earnestly knock, so admittance to the lessons of Freemasonry are opened by the proper knock at the Inner Door of the Lodge.

Innocence

From time immemorial, the lamb has been regarded as an emblem of innocence. Since Masons are required to strive after perfect innocence, especially in the Masonic conduct, the apron worn by them must be made of pure white lambskin.

Installation

Stallum was the Late Latin for place, or seat, or proper position, which meaning is preserved in our English "stall." To "install" therefore means that one has been placed in his seat or station—the "in" meaning here the same as in English. A Masonic installation is a ceremony by which an elected officer is officially placed in the seat to which his brethren have elected him.

Interment

the act or ritual of interring or burying.The grave is the natural resting place for the bodies of the dead, but it is not the final abode of the spirit. We honor our dead in interment, but we await their Resurrection.

Invest

to give; to furnish; to clothe

Inviolate

not broken or disregarded; not told to others; respected Light knowledge or understanding

Ionic

one of the three classical (Greek) orders of architecture, originated in an area of ancient Greece known as Ionia

Iron Tools

In order that perfect quiet and reverence might prevail in the building of the Temple of Solomon, no iron tool of any kind was employed.

J

Jachin

The two great pillars of Solomon's Temple support-ing the Great Porch, known as Solomon's Porch, were called Boaz and Jachin. Jachin is a combination of two words, *Jah*, the poetical name of Jehovah, and *iachin*, meaning establishment. The full significance of the name is, therefore, "With God's help to establish," the sym-bolical meaning given to in the work of Freemasonry.

Jacob's Ladder

The story of Jacob's dream or vision is which he saw a stair-way leading from earth to Heaven and angels descending and ascending on it holds an important place in Masonic ritual. It is employed as a symbol of the progressive course from earth to Heaven, and of the transition from death to life.

Jah

the poetical name of Jehovah.

Japhet

the eldest son of Noah. It is said that the first ark — the Ark of Safety, the archetype of the Tabernacle — was constructed by Shem, Ham, and Japhet under the superintendence of Noah. Hence these are significant words to the Royal Arch Mason.

Jesus and the Temple

Jesus was carried to the Temple when he was only forty days old for purification ceremonies. Again at twelve, for Passover in Jerusalem and later for public ministry.

Judah

Judah, the fourth son of Jacob and the founder of the tribe bearing his name, is also the representative of a key point in ancient Masonry. Judah distinguished himself on a number of occasions and was given Messianic distinction in the tribal blessings of his father and by Moses. The royal house of Israel was of the tribe of Judah, even as was Jesus. The tribe of Judah was the first to cross the Jordan and enter the Promised Land. For this reason, and because of its distinction as the tribe of David, Solomon and Jesus, Judah represents or symbolizes the entrance of the candidate into the Light and liberty of Freemasonry.

Judicious

having, exercising or characterized by sound judgement; discrete; wise

Junior Past Master

a Mason who served as Master of a lodge the year before.

Junior Warden

The "Third in Command" of a lodge. Similar to "Second Vice-President" in other organizations.

K

Kadosh

In the AASR, this is the 30th degree. The word is Hebrew, and signifies holy or consecrated, and is thus intended to denote the elevated character of the Degree and the sublimity of the truths which distinguish it and its possessors from the other Degrees. The Degree of Kadosh, though found in many of the Rites and in various countries, seems, in all of them, to have been more or less connected with the Knights Templar.

Keepers of the House Shall Tremble

This expression is a figure of the failings of the body in old age or as weakened by the approach of death. The usual interpretation is that the arms and legs are the keepers.

Keystone

The stone placed in the center of an arch which preserves the others in their places, and secures firmness and stability to the arch. As it was formerly the custom of Operative Masons to place a peculiar mark on each stone of a building to designate the workman by whom it had been adjusted, so the Keystone was most likely to receive the most prominent mark, that of the Superintendent of the structure.

Kilwinning

As the city of York claims to be the birthplace of Freemasonry in England, the obscure little village of Kilwinning is entitled to the same honor with respect to the origin of Freemasonry in Scotland.

L

Labor

The Latin *labor* meant toil, work, the putting forth of effort; it appears to be akin to *robur*, or strength, preserved in our "robust." While labor and work are used interchangeably, the latter is a more generic word, and admits of a much wider range of uses. Work may be either hard or easy but labor is always hard; work is used of all sorts of effort; labor refers generally to muscular effort, followed by fatigue. When labor is kept up unremittingly it is toil; and when toil is uninteresting, uninspiring, and poorly paid it is drudgery. When working, one's ambition is to succeed with it; when laboring, one looks forward to resting from it; hence, it is from labor that we seek refreshment, not from work.

Landmark

In ancient times, it was customary to mark the boundaries of lands by the means of stone pillars or heaps of stones. The removal of such landmarks was a grievous crime and an evidence of fraudulent intent by the offender. In speculative Masonry there are also landmarks, and the same rigid rule with reference to ancient landmarks applies to these. The landmarks of Masonry are those principles by which the Craft is bounded, that is, marked off from all other societies and associations and without which it would lose its identity.

Lay or Inlay

The manner or position in which something is situated (lay). To set (a piece of wood, metal, etc.) into a surface to form a design that is usually level with the surface (inlay).

Legend

The Greeks had *legein*, speak; the Latins *legere*, read; from these we have legend, lecture, etc. In the early Christian church the legend was the Scripture selection read in a church service; later the term became applied to stories about the lives of the saints, especially to their wonders and miracles. The famous "Golden Legend," a collection of such stories, was one of the most popular books of the Middle Ages. Legend, as now used, is a story without historical foundations but told in the form of history, hence our "Legend of the Third Degree," a narrative in dramatic form that Masons have long understood to be non-historical.

Level of Equality

The level in Masonry is a symbol of the fraternal equality of mankind as the offspring of God, all races and nations having been made of one blood. The fundamental principle that all men are created equal, with certain inalienable rights to life, liberty and the pursuit of happiness is basic in Freemasonry. We meet upon the "level" because Masonic rights, duties, and privileges are the same for all members without distinction.

Lewis

A candidate for the Degrees of Masonry whose father is a Master Mason. In the same sense, the French use *louveteau*.

The operative tool known as the *lewis* was an iron clamp capable of exerting outward pressure when inserted in a cavity in the top of a stone. By that means, a stone could be raised and put in place with no chains or clamps on the outside to interfere with the setting of it. The clamp was then released and the lewis withdrawn. The

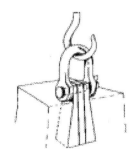

transferal of this term to symbolic use has been the subject of some speculation. It is said that as the lewis is used to assist in the lifting of stones, so the Lewis assists and supports the father. The term appears in the English Constitutions of 1738 near the close of the Deputy Grand Master's song.

Libertine

Liber was the Latin for "free," as in our liberty, liberal, etc. When the Romans gave a slave his freedom he was called *libertus*, so that in Roman history a libertine was a freedman. In theology a libertine came to mean one who holds loose views in regard to morality, a immoral person who flouts moral laws. The early Freemasons employed the later use of the word.

Light

Throughout the ritual and work of Freemasonry, Light is the symbol of knowledge, and just as God spoke into existence physical light, so He is the original source of all true knowledge. The Great Light of Masonry is His inspired work. Masons are pledged to strive after more and more Light as life goes on and should seek above all things Light Eternal. By an inevitable association the word came into metaphorical use to mean the coming of truth and knowledge into the mind. When a candidate ceases to be ignorant of Masonry, when through initiation the truths of Masonry have found entrance into his mind, he is said to be "enlightened" in the Masonic sense.

Light of Life

The source of enlightenment and knowledge for life's darkness, perplexities and doubts, as well as for life's responsibilities and duties, is the Holy Bible — the Great Light of Masonry.

Lily Work

The lily is an emblem of peace and purity. For this reason, lily work occupied a place of conspicuousness and distinction in the ornamentations of the Temple and its furniture.

Lion of the Tribe of Judah

In the tribal benediction pronounced upon Judah, the "lion's whelp" is used emblematically of strength. Hence, the ensign on the banner of Judah was a lion. The phrase in the Masonic ritual, "The lion of the tribe of Judah," is Messianic and refers to Christ.

Lodge

This word comes from the Old French, English and Medieval Latin, and meant generally a hut, a cottage, a gallery, a covered way, etc.; our "lobby" had the same beginning. How the Operative Masons came to employ the term, and just what they meant by it, has never been determined; they had a symbolic Lodge, their building was a Lodge, the group of members was a Lodge, an assembly of Masons was a Lodge, and often times the whole body of Masons was called a Lodge. In our own usage the word has three technical meanings; the place where Masons meet, the assembly of the brethren duly congregated for labor, and a piece of furniture.

Lost Word

The lost word was the ineffable name of God, but the term is used symbolically of Divine Truth.

M

Manual

relating to the hand, from the Latin *manus*, a hand.

Mason

This is a word from the Middle Ages, with an uncertain origin. The old Gothic *maitan* meant to hew, or cut, and it is supposed the word carried that general meaning through Medieval Latin, English, German, and in the Scandinavian languages. If at first it was used only of a stone-cutter, it came later to mean a builder. Why the Operatives were called "Freemasons" is still an unsolved puzzle; the most likely view is that they were a society of builders free to move from one place to another in contrast to the gild Masons who were confined in their labors to one community. In our Fraternity a Mason is a builder of manhood and brotherhood.

Masonic age

the symbolic *Masonic age* corresponds to the different degrees obtained by the Mason. For a Master Mason, his Masonic age is three.

Masonic regalia

aprons, jewels, implements and hats appropriate to one's station or office.

Master

The Latin root *mag* had the general meaning of great — as in "magnitude"; it was the source of the Latin magister, head, chief, principal, the word of which "magistrate" was made. During the Middle Ages it fell into use as a conventional title applied to persons in superior rank, preserved in our own familiar "mister," always written "Mr," a colloquial form of "master." Also it came to be used of a man who had overcome the difficulties in learning an art, thereby proving himself to be greater than his task, as when it is said of an artist who has overcome all the obstacles and difficulties of painting, "He is a master." A Master Mason is so called because be has proved himself capable of mastering the work; also because he belongs to a Degree so named.

Master of the Lodge

This title signifies "teacher," not Lord. The Master of the Lodge should be well informed in the mysteries, symbols, allegories and principles of Freemasonry. Masonry is a science of morals, clothed in symbols and any Brother who becomes a teacher of this science must fully understand the allegories in which it is enveloped, the symbolisms with which it is illustrated, the myths and legends of Masonry, and their mystical applications to everyday life. What the sun is by day to the world, the Master is to the Lodge.

Master Builder

In the material realm, a master builder is one who is qualified in intellect and training to do constructive building of symmetrical and perfect order — an architect, skilled worker and capable artisan. Hiram Abif, the widow's son of the tribe of Naphtali, was such a master builder. With the very best materials furnished him by King Solomon, he carried to completion an edifice of magnificence and superlative beauty and glory. In speculative Masonry, a master builder is one who is qualified in heart and mind, by skill in moral and spiritual science, and by Holy consecration to erect temples of immortal characters.

Mercenary

motivated solely by a desire for monetary or material gain.

Metal Tools

In ancient Israel, the use of metal tools in the actual construction of sacred altars and edifices was forbidden; hence, the preparation of all materials for the building of Solomon's Temple was done in the forests and quarries.

Money Changers

These were exchange bankers who set up tables in the precincts of the Temple where they provided Jewish coins for Temple offerings in exchange for foreign moneys, charging fees for their services. Jesus drove them from the Temple, declaring that they had made the "House of Prayer a den of thieves."

Monitor

The Latin *monere* meant to warn; it was the root of our admonish, admonition, etc.; a monitor was the man who did the warning. The term became widely used in early school systems of the senior pupils in a class whose duty it was to instruct his juniors; from this it passed to include the book, the blackboard and other instruments used by him in his teachings. Our use of it carries this last meaning; the Masonic Monitor is a book for teaching a candidate the exoteric work.

Mosaic

This word has nothing to do with Moses. Its root was the Greek *mousa*, a muse, suggesting something artistic. The same root appears in our "museum," literally a place where artistic work is exhibited. Through the Latin it came into  modern languages and during the Middle Ages became narrowed down to mean a pattern formed by small pieces of inlay, a form of decorative work much in vogue during the time of the Operative Masons. Our mosaic pavement is so called because it consists of an inlay pattern, small black and white squares alternating to suggest day and night.

Mother Lodge

The lodge in which one is made a Mason. The first lodge to which a Mason joined, regardless of how many other lodges he joins.

Mouth to Ear

The Freemason is taught by an expressive symbol, to whisper good counsel in his Brother's ear, and to warn him of approaching danger. "It is a rare thing," says Bacon, "except it be from a perfect and entire friend, to have counsel given that is not bowed and crooked to some ends which he hath that giveth it." And hence it is an admirable lesson, which Freemasonry here teaches us, to use the lips and the tongue only in the service of a Brother.

Mystic Tie

This phrase refers to the bond of fraternal love, to the solemn vows of eternal Masonry, irrespective of differences in race, nationality and conflicting interests. By this mystic tie, men of the most discordant opinions are united in one band, meet at one altar, even when fighting in opposing armies or affiliated with different religions. It is, indeed, an indefinable spiritual tie, and those under its influence are rightly spoken of as "Brethrenof the Mystic Tie."

N

Names of the Temple

The Temple built by Solomon, which occupies such importance throughout the symbolisms and legends of Freemasonry, is given a number of names in the Bible: The Palace of Jehovah, The House of Sanctuary, and The House of Ages.

Naphtali

Naphtali was the fifth son of Jacob and the founder of the tribe bearing his name. In the tribal blessing given him by his father, and confirmed by Moses, wise counsel and prosperity were to be the chief characteristics of the tribe. Naphtali represents the investiture of the lambskin apron bestowed in the West and South.

Noah

In all the old Masonic manuscript Constitutions that are extant, Noah and the Flood play an important part in the Legend of the Craft. Hence, as the Masonic system became developed, the Patriareh was looked upon as what was called a Patron of Freemasonry.

North Side

In Masonic symbolism the North Side of the Lodge represents God's exalted throne.

Northeast Corner

As one progresses through the rites and symbolisms of Freemasonry, receiving more and more Light, he reaches the Northeast Corner with all the outward appearances of a perfect and upright Mason, a true and tried representative of the cornerstone of a great moral and spiritual edifice.

Notice

a call issued by the Secretary, by order of the Lodge or Master, or by other competent authority to attend or perform as specified. A notice is not the same as a *Summons*.

O

Obligation

From time immemorial, men have entered into covenants of brotherhood and friendship under solemn obligations of fidelity and loyalty, and whenever the circumstances and purposes warranted it, secrecy has been pledged. This practice among Masons has many precedents and is based on the truths and principles set forth of the Great Light of Masonry. All obligations voluntarily taken in Masonry must be faithfully performed and are never subject to revocation. The obligation is the tie, or bond, itself; in Masonry a formal and voluntary pledge on the candidate's part by virtue of which he is accepted as a responsible member of the family of Masons.

Oblong

This has long been a puzzle word in Masonic nomenclature. How, it is asked, can a square be oblong, when a square is equal on all its sides? The answer is that in this connection "square" is used in the sense of rectangle; the angles are squared, not the sides. Oblong is derived from *ob*, near, or before, and *longus*, long; that is, it means something approximately long, so that the main axis is much longer than the others, as a slender leaf, a shaft, etc. An "oblong square" is a rectangle of which two opposite sides are much longer than the other two. The Lodge symbolically is an oblong square in this sense.

Opening of the Lodge

It is absolutely necessary that the Lodge be opened in due and ancient form. Without these ceremonies, the assembly is not a Masonic Lodge. This is true because the Master must be reminded of the dignity and character of himself and of his position. And the other officers must be impressed with the respect and veneration due from their sundry stations. But more important, the Fraternity in Lodge assembly and in work must maintain a reverential awe for Deity, and must look to the Great Light of Freemasonry, the Holy Bible, for guidance and instruction. Thus, in the opening of the Lodge, the Great Architect of the Universe must be worshipped, and His blessings upon the work about to be performed must be supplicated. At the same time, prayer is offered for peace and harmony in the closing of the Lodge.

Operative

We distinguish Operative Masons, builders of the Middle Ages, founders of Masonry, from Spectulative Masons, present members of the Fraternity, using the builders' tools as emblems and symbols. The Latin for toil, or work, was *opus*, still used in that form in English to signify a musical or literary achievement. *Opus* was the root of *operari*, to work, whence we have our operate, operative, operation, opera, operator, and many others. The Operative Mason was one who toiled at building in the plain, literal sense of the word. "Speculative" will be explained farther in this publication.

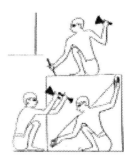

Ordo ab chao

Latin for: *Order from chaos*. This phrase is normally associated with the Scottish Rite.

Ornament

Ornare was the Latin verb meaning to adorn, to equip, of which the noun was *amamen* turn, trappings, embellishment, furniture, etc., from which was derived our "adornment" and "ornament." In church usage "ornaments" was the name given to all the equipment used in the services of divine worship. We speak of the mosaic pavement, the indented tessel, and blazing star as "ornaments of the Lodge;" whether the term was used by Lodges originally because they were considered to be adornments, or because they were part of the Lodge equipment it is impossible to say, though the latter alternative appears to be the more likely.

P

Passions

great emotion; the emotions as distinguished from reason; powerful or compelling feelings or desires.

Password

The Latin *passus* meant pace, step, track, passage; it contains the picture of a path, road, aisle, or door through which one can make his way, hence our "pass," derived from it. From it also we have our word "pace." A password is any agreed word or counter-sign that permits one to pass through an entrance or passage otherwise closed.

Peace on Earth

The principles and tenets of Freemasonry teach "peace on earth and good will to men."

Pearly Gates

The splendor and beauty and glory of Solomon's Temple and of its appointments were but symbols and prophecies of the superior Temple, that house not made with hands, eternal in the Heavens, with its gates of pearl.

Pectoral

belonging to the breast; from the Latin *pectus*, the breast.

Pedal

belonging to the feet, from the Latin *pedes*, the feet.

Penalty

It is significant that our "penal" derives from the Latin for pain, *paena*, the root of our penance, penalty, penitence, penitentiary, punish, primitive, pine, and a circle of similar English words. It has the meaning of pain inflicted for the purpose of correction, discipline, or protecting society, never the infliction of pain for its own sake. Our own penalties are symbolical in form, their language being derived from early English forms of punishment for heresy and treason.

Perfect Points of Entrance

symbolic action called for on entrance into a lodge. Every Mason has four perfect points of entrance which are beautifully illustrated in the four Cardinal Virtues: Temperance, Fortitude, Prudence, and Justice.

Pillar

The Latin *pila* was a pile, — such as a pile under a house — a pier, a pillar, or a mole, — the last named a massive stonework enclosing a harbor. In ancient times pillars were used for all manner of religious and symbolical purposes, as when Jacob erected a pillar at a grave, or Solomon set up two great pillars — the prototype of ours — on the Porch before his Temple.

Pillars of Brass

Important and significant features of the architecture of King Solomon's Temple were two giant bronze shafts which stood in striking relief in front of the entrance to the Great Porch at the east entrance of the Temple, one on the left and one on the right. Each was seventy feet high and twenty-four feet in circumference. They were highly ornamented by a network of brass overhung with wreaths of bronze pomegranates, each row containing one hundred. Each of these giant pillars had a chapiter at the top, ten feet in length, making the total height of each pillar eighty feet. On the top of these chapiters were great bowls for oil, called pommels, over which were hung festoon-like wreaths of pomegranates, interspersed at various points with lily work. These two great shafts were given the names Boaz and Jachin.

Pillars of Wisdom

The seven great pillars of wisdom are regarded by Masons to be of superlative worth in the building of a moral and spiritual edifice.

Pitcher Be Broken at the Fountain

The heart is the fountain of human life, and the great vein which carries the blood to the right ventricle is symbolically called the pitcher. When this is broken as a result of the decrepitude of old age or by human disease, death soon follows.

Plumb

Plumbum was the Latin for lead, and was used also of a scourge with a blob of lead tied to it, of a line with a lead ball at its end for testing perpendicularity, etc., the source of our plumb, plumber, plunge, plump, plumbago, plummet, etc. A plumb-line is accordingly a line, or cord, with a piece of lead at the bottom to pull it taut, used to test vertical walls with the line of gravity, hence, by a simple expansion of reference, an emblem of uprightness.

Up means up, right means straight; an upright man

is one who stands straight up and down, doesn't bend or wabble, has no crooks in him, like a good solid wall that won't cave in under pressure.

Poor

Almost from the moment that a candidate for Freemasonry crosses the threshold of the Lodge, the duty of rendering aid and sustenance to those who lack in this world's necessities is urged upon him.

Porch

The Great Porch of the Temple of Solomon was magnificent and expansive, and its value to the appointments and uses of the Temple was invaluable. Hence, this porch is given a distinctive recognition in the ritual and teachings of Masonry.

Pot of Incense, The

is an emblem of a pure heart, which is always an acceptable sacrifice to the Deity; and, as this glows with fervent heat, so should our hearts continually glow with gratitude to the great and beneficent Author of our existence, for the manifold blessings and comforts we enjoy.

Prayer

Petitions to Deity in behalf on one's own needs, intercessions for others, communion with God, and prayer in all its elements of praise and worship are fundamentals in the tenets of Freemasonry. From the time a candidate crosses the threshold of the Lodge to the topmost Degree in Masonry, the privilege and duty of prayer are urged upon him, and every step is taken in a Holy atmosphere of Divine worship.

Preparation

In all the work of Freemasonry, emphasis is placed upon the importance of adequate preparation of moral, ethical and spiritual vocations. Preparation of the heart is the first essential in Masonry, and certain outward preparations symbolic of, and manifesting, inward preparedness are required.

Profane

This has a technical meaning in Masonry, nevertheless it adheres closely to the original significance of the word. *Fanum* was the Latin for temple; pro meant "before," in the sense of "outside of." It is the picture of man standing on the outside, not permitted to enter. It has this same sense in Masonry; the "profane" are those men and women who stand outside of Masonry. The word here, of course, has nothing to do with profanity in the sense of sacrilegious language.

Prudence

Growing out of the cardinal virtues which are emphasized throughout the degrees of Masonry is the practice of prudence by which we are instructed to regulate our conduct by the dictates of reason and in obedience to the cardinal virtues of faith, hope and love.

Q

Qualification

Qualify comes from the same word as quality. The root of it is the Latin *qua*, preserved in our "what." The quality of a thing was its *whatness*, the stuff of which it was made, its nature. The *fy* in "qualify" is from *facere*, to make, so that "qualify" means that a thing is made of the required stuff; and qualification means the act by which a thing is made of the required nature, or is declared to have it. The candidate for the Degrees of Masonry must possess certain characteristics in his nature; must be a man of lawful age, etc., and these are his qualifications.

Quarry

The Latin *quadratum* was a square; originally, quadrate and quarry meant the same. The word became applied to the pit from which rock is hewn because the principal task of workmen therein was to cut, or square, the stones; hence, literally a quarry is a place where stone-squaring is done. In Masonry "quarry" sometimes refers to the rock pits from which Solomon's workmen hewed out the stones for his Temple; at other times it refers to the various arenas of Masonic activities, as when it is said of an active Lodge member that "he is a faithful laborer in the quarry."

Quorum

Parliamentary law provides that a deliberative Body shall not proceed to business until a quorum of its members is present. This law is generally applicable to Freemasonry. According to common ritualistic rules, seven constitute a quorum, for work or business, in an Entered Apprentice's Lodge, five in a Fellow Craft's, and three in a Master Mason's. In addition, many lodges require that that either the Master or one Warden be present before a lodge can open.

R

Raised

In the Anglo Saxon *arisan* was used for any motion up or down, but in English it became used only of an upward motion, as in arise, rising, raise, rear, etc. Raise means to hoist, or carry, or lift, a body upward in space. There is no need to explain to a Mason why it is said of a candidate who has completed the Third Degree that he has been "raised," or why the climactic ceremony in that Degree is described as "raising." One is "initiated" an Entered Apprentice, "passed" a Fellowcraft, "raised" a Master Mason.

Refreshment

Friscus, or *frescus*, in the Latin had the meaning of new, fresh, recent; the *re* meant again; so that refresh means to renew, to make over, to undo the ravages of use and time, in Shakespeare's phrase, "to knit up the raveled sleeve of care." To "pass from labor to refreshment" is to find rest and recreation so as to undo the wearing effects of toil, as when a laborer knocks off at noon to eat his lunch and have a rest.

Regular

The Latin *rex*, king, sovereign, ruler, was a root from which many words have sprung, regal, royal, etc.; the Latins themselves had *regula*, or rule, and *regere*, to rule or govern. From this source has come our "regular." It means a rule established on legitimate authority. In Masonry "regular" is applied to those rules which have been established by Grand Lodges and Grand Masters. A "regular Lodge" is one that conforms to Grand Lodge requirements; a "regular Mason" is the member of such a Lodge who conforms to its laws and bylaws.

Relief

To relieve the distressed is a duty incumbent on all men, but particularly on Masons, who are linked together by an indissoluble chain of sincere affection. To soothe the unhappy, to sympathize with their misfortunes, to compassionate their miseries, and to restore peace to their troubled minds, is the great aim we have in view. On this basis we form our friendships and establish our connections.

Reverence for God

The very nature of God, His attributes and qualities, His creation, preservation and sovereignty over man, His redemptive grace and love, even His name, demands of man a reverent attitude at all times. God, Himself, and His name which stands for his personality, supremacy, majesty and glory are always revered in the Lodge of Masons, and the same attitude toward God should characterize the personal life of every true Mason. Anything and everything that represents God to the mind of man should be held sacred.

Right

This, one of the noblest words in the English language, is also one of the oldest, being found in the very ancient Sanskrit in the form *raj* meaning rule. It appeared in Latin as *rectus*, meaning direct, straight, a rule, — rule being used in the sense of our ruler, a device for drawing a line which is the shortest distance between two points. Such words as regent, rail, direct, rector, rectify, rule, came from this Latin term. Right means "straight," as in a "right line," a "right angle," etc.; through a familiar metaphorical application it has come to stand for conduct in conformity with moral law. Our "rights" are those privileges which strict law allows to us. A "horizontal" is a right line on the level; a "perpendicular" is a right line up and down, or at right angles to the horizontal. "Right" and "regular," discussed just above, originally were close together in meaning.

Rite

a system of Masonry beginning in the craft lodge and concluding in a final degree. A arrangement of Masonic degrees. "Rite," like "right," is very old; it has been traced to the if Sanskrit *riti*, meaning usage, which in turn was derived from *ri*, meaning flow, suggesting the regular current of river. In Latin this became *ritus* meaning in general a custom, more particularly a religious custom, or usage. Masonry has had many rites, some existing for only a short period of time.

Ritual

In Masonry the ritual is the prescribed set of ceremonies used for the purpose of initiation. It should be noted that a set of ceremonies does not become a ritual until it has been prescribed by some official authority, as a Grand Lodge.

Royal Art, The

the art of building in former times (architecture); it is used today as to designate Freemasonry as well.

S

Sabbath Day

Freemasonry recognizes man's constitutional requirement for one day's rest from the ordinary secular toils of life, and accepts as part of its fundamental teachings of the Divine establishment of the Sabbath Day. By legendary instructions, through symbolisms, and by precept, the privilege and duty of Sabbath observations are inculcated. The Sabbath Day is honored as an allotted period for rest and Divine Worship.

Saints John

Saint John the Baptist and Saint John the Evangelist are the two patron saints of Freemasonry in the USA.

Sanctuary

Holy places dedicated to the services and worship of God are a necessity for man. They are to be revered even as the name of God and utilized by man for his spiritual culture and for communion with the Most High. Moses erected a Sanctuary under the directions of God, and Holy places for worship have been perpetuated ever since. In the Bible, this name is ascribed to the Most Holy Place in the Tabernacle and in the Temple.

Sanctum Sanctorum

the Latin phrase referring to the Holy of Holies or innermost chamber of King Solomon's Temple where the Ark of the Covenant was kept.

Scottish Rite

a 33 degree system created in 1801 in Charleston, South Carolina and came to be known as the Ancient and Accepted Scottish Rite. While the system has 33 degrees, it is normally worked in the U.S. from the 4th to 33rd degree. Only a very few craft lodges in the U.S. work in this ritual (mostly in Louisiana). Outside the U.S. it is a very popular ritual used in craft lodges and well as the bodies working the higher degrees of the rite.

Scripture Readings

It is not only required that the VSL on the altar in the Lodge be spread open as a necessary preparation for opening the Lodge and during its work, but that it be opened at certain passages during the several Degrees. For the First Degree, the assigned passage is normally Psalms 133; for the Second, Amos, chapter 7; in some jurisdictions, 1 Corinthians, chapter 13, and for the Third, Ecclesiastes, chapter 12.

Seal

This, like our words "sign" and "insignia," is derived from the Latin *sigillum*, diminutive of *signum*, meaning a mark, or sign. It is some kind of device affixed to a document in place of a signature or in close connection with a signature for the purpose of showing that the document is regular or official. A document bearing the seal of a Lodge shows that it is officially issued by the Lodge, and not by some irresponsible person or persons. The word is also used for the tool by means the device is stamped into wax, or whatever similar material may be used for the purpose.

Secrecy

From *Se*, apart, and *cernere*, separate, the Latins had *secretum*, suggesting something separated from other things, apart from common knowledge, hidden, covered, isolated, hence "secrecy." There is a fundamental difference between "secret" and "hidden," far whereas the latter may mean that nobody knows where a thing is, nothing can be secret without at least one person knowing it. The secrets of Freemasonry are known to all Masons, therefore are not hidden; they are secrets only in the sense that they are not known to profanes. A similar word is "occult," which means a thing naturally secret, one, as it were, that secretes itself, so that few can know about it. See also the paragraphs on "clandestine" and "mystery" in the preceding pages. There is also another less familiar word in Masonry meaning hidden, covered up, concealed, secret; it is pronounced "hail" but is spelled "hele."

Secretary

The present use of this word has departed widely from its original meaning. The Latin *secretus* meant secret, private; *secretarium* was a conclave, a caucus, a council behind closed doors, consequently a *secretarius* was some very confidential officer, and was used of a secretary in our sense, of a notary, a scribe, etc. Since the handling of correspondence and the keeping of records is usually a confidential service the man who does it has come to be called a secretary. The secretary of a Lodge cares for all its correspondence and its records.

Self Support

the duty of supporting one's self and his family by individual initiative and personal labor is a universal tenet of Freemasonry.

Senior Warden

The "Second in Command" of a lodge. Similar to "First Vice-President" in other organizations.

Shibboleth

A word used by followers of Jephthah to test certain of the Ephraimites who sought to escape across the Jordan after having refused to fight in the armies of Israel was *Shibboleth*. Because of their Ephraimite dialect, they pronounced it *Sibboleth*.

Shod

wearing footgear, with shoes on, not barefoot

Sideliner

a Mason who, when attending a Masonic meeting, is not sitting as an Officer of the Lodge.

Sign

This comes from the Latin *signum*, a word which appears in a dozen or more English words, as signature, signet, signify, consign, countersign, resign, etc. Where a seal is used principally on documents and for the purpose of showing them to be official, sign is used much more variously and widely; it is some kind of gesture, device, mark, or design which indicates something, or points to something, and which often has a meaning known only to the initiated. Masonic signs are gestures that convey a meaning which only Masons understand, and which most frequently are used for purposes of recognition.

Silver Cord

"Or ever the silver cord be loosed" is a figurative expression in the beautiful passage descriptive of the delibitations of old age or approaching death. It is thought to refer to the weakening of the spinal cord which results in the loosening of the nervous system.

Solomon

Solomon was the son of David and Bathsheba, and David's successor on the throne of Israel. Though not the oldest of David's sons, he was chosen by his father to be his successor and was crowned king prior to David's death, when only about twenty-one years of age. He was solemnly charged by his father to build the Temple for which large funds had already been gathered. Solomon prayed especially for wisdom which was given to him by God above the measure of any other man in history. The league made with Hiram, King of Tyre, by his father was perpetuated, and by his assistance the Temple was carried to completion within seven and one-half years, beginning the fourth year of his reign.

Speculative

The Latin *specere* meant to see, to look about; *specula* was a watchtower, so called because from it one could look about over a wide territory. It came to be used metaphorically of the mental habit of noting all the aspects of a subject; also, as applied to theoretical knowledge as opposed to practical skill. "Speculative Masonry" was knowledge of the science, or theory, of building; "Operative Masonry," trained skill in putting that knowledge into practice. When Operative Masonry was dropped out of the Craft in the eighteenth century, only the speculative elements remained and these became the basis of our present Fraternity. It is for this reason that we continue to describe it as Speculative Masonry. The word has nothing to do with philosophical speculation, or with theorizing merely for its own sake.

Spiritual Temple

Freemasonry draws many sublime lessons and deduces many worthy truths from the symbolisms of the building of King Solomon's Temple, as well as from operative Masonry and architecture respecting the more important superstructure of moral, ethical and spiritual components knows as the Spiritual Temple. The building of this Temple is in vain without Divine aid. It fact, it must be built with God as the Chief Architect, and all the material that goes into it must pass His inspection and approval.

Square

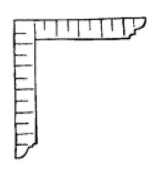

The Latin *quad ratum* was a square. *Quatuor* meant "four;" from it we have square, four, quad, quadrangle, squadron, etc. In geometry a square is a four-sided straight-lined figure having all its sides equal and all its angles right angles; and since early carpenters and Masons had to use an instrument for proving the angles to be right, they fell into the habit of calling that instrument a square. In Masonry the square is used in at least three distinct senses; as a sharp instrument, as a working tool, and as a symbol, the last named when used with the compasses on the Holy Bible. As a symbol it refers to the earth, for so long a time supposed to be square in shape; as a working tool, it refers to all those forces by means of which one prepares himself to fit into his own proper place in the Brotherhood, like a Perfect Ashlar in a wall.

Stand To and Abide By

This is a unique pledge of every mason and means that he binds himself to stand by and obey every regulation of the Order, that he will be governed at all times by its laws and rules, and that the landmarks of the Fraternity will be followed faithfully in every detail.

Steward

This came into general use through the church, in which it was adopted as the name for an important official and also for an important theological doctrine; the doctrine of stewardship. The word itself had a peculiar origin. In Anglo Saxon *stigo* was a sty or place in which domestic animals were kept; a *weard* (see "warden") was a guard, or keeper; therefore the steward was the keeper of the cattle pens. Its meaning became enlarged to include the duties of general over-seer, one who is in charge of a household or estate for another; and still more generally, one who provides for the needs for food, money, and supplies. In the history of Masonry the office of steward has performed a variety of functions; the caring of funds, distribution of charity, preparing for banquets and similar services.

Subdue

to quiet or bring under control by physical force or persuasion; to reduce the intensity or degree of; tone down.

Sublime

Sublimis, in Latin, referred to something high, lofty, exalted, like a city set on top of a hill, or an eagle's nest atop some lonely crag. It refers to that which is eminent, of superlative degree, moral grandeur, spiritual exaltation. Inasmuch as the Third Degree is at the top of the system of Ancient Craft Masonry, it is known as "The Sublime Degree."

Superfluity

overabundance; excess; immoderate, especially living habits or desires.

Summons

Like the word *monitor*, explained some pages back, summons is derived from the Latin term of which the verb was *monere*, meaning to warn, or to remind, as in "admonish"; the "sum" is the combining form of *sub*, under, or privy to, in the secret of, as in the old phrase "sub rosa." A summons is an official call sent out by persons in authority to some person acknowledging that authority to appear at some place, or to perform some duty; in other words a person who is "on the inside," who is a member, is admonished by his superiors, and must obey under penalty. The duty involved and the penalty attached distinguishes a summons from a mere invitation. A Lodge, Grand Lodge, or some official issues a summons; a Mason is under obligation to respond to either, if it be due, official, or regular.

Superstructure

anything based on, or rising from, some foundation or basis; an entity, concept or complex based on a more fundamental one.

Sword Pointing to a Naked Heart

The "Sword Pointing to a Naked Heart" demonstrates that justice will sooner or later overtake us; and although our thoughts, words, and actions may be hidden from the eyes of man, yet that the All-Seeing Eye, whom the sun, moon, and stars obey, and under Whose watchful care, even comets perform their stupendous revolutions, pervades the inmost recesses of the human heart, and will reward us according to our merits.

Symbol

It is interesting to compare this word with "emblem" with which it is so often confused. The Greek *symbolon* was a mark, or sign, or token, or tally; it is derived from sun, together, and *ballein*, put, or throw, from which we have ball, ballistics, etc. *Symbolon* indicated two things put together, thrown together, or matched together. If, for example, the numeral 9 is matched to a pile of marbles, one to one, the 9 is a symbol of the number of marbles. From this came the custom of calling a symbol some object, device, design, picture, etc., used not for its own sake, but for the purpose of referring to some other, and perhaps very different, thing with which it has been associated. It is any visible, audible, or tangible object used to typify some idea, or truth, or quality, as when a wedding ring is made the symbol of marriage, the square is made the symbol of the earth, or the cross is made the symbol of Christianity, the crescent of Mohammedanism, etc.

T

Tabernacle

This was a moveable structure built under the directions of Moses at Mount Sinai according to the pattern given to him by God in a special revelation. In its truest sense, the Tabernacle was a representation of the presence of God in the midst of Israel, and the central place for worship. This is the model Solomon used to build his Temple.

Table of Shewbread

This article of furniture in the Tabernacle was a table made of acacia wood and of the ordinary make-up with legs. It was furnished with dishes, bowls, spoons and covers, all made of pure gold. Upon this table was placed twelve cakes of bread made of fine flour, in two rows of six cakes, called shewbread (also referred to shewbread). These cakes or loaves were removed every Sabbath and fresh bread supplied in their place. Only the priests were allowed to eat this removed bread. In King Solomon's Temple, instead of just one table, ten were used. They were patterned after the table of the Tabernacle, except they were made of pure gold and were much larger.

Temple

King Solomon's Temple holds a place of universal and pre-eminent interest due, in great measure, to Freemasonry which has kept alive through the centuries many fascinating legends and romances, innumerable symbols and rituals, a goodly number of rites and ceremonies associated with the building of the Temple and with its history. It is interesting to note that in Masonic nomenclature the ideal life, here and hereafter, is described metaphorically as a temple, one of a thousand examples of the extent to which Freemasonry is saturated with religious language and emotions.

Temple Builder

The legend of the Temple builder which forms a significant feature of the Third Degree in Freemasonry and the basis of profound lectures has been an essential part of Masonic ritual and Degree work throughout the history of the Order. Its authenticity cannot be questioned nor can its importance in the rites of Freemasonry be overestimated.

Temple of the Body

The symbolism of Solomon's Temple in the science of speculative Masonry, and the several rites of the Order based upon operative Masonry in the construction of the Temple, are intended to convey and inculcate great moral, ethical and spiritual truths. Among these truths is the teaching that man's body is to be made a fit Temple for the indwelling of God, and than many of the symbolisms in the building of King Solomon's Temple find their realities in human life and experience.

Temperance

moderation in action, thought or feeling; self-restraint; a habitual moderation in the indulgence of the appetites or passions; moderation in, or abstinence from, the use of intoxicating substances.

Ten Commandments

Masons recognize and honor the Decalogue incorporated in the laws of Moses as being of Divine origin and accept them as the moral code by which all human relations with God and with mankind should be regulated.

Testimony

Evidence in support of a fact or assertion; proof. In ancient Israel and other societies, the putting off of the shoes was a testimony of reverence for God or for an earthly superior, and as a token of confirmation in making contracts with fellowmen. The practice in certain rituals of Masonry may be traced back to this ancient custom.

Three Chambers

The upper, middle and lower chambers of King Solomon's Temple were rooms adjoining the main building fitted for quiet communication with God, as places for the preparation of priests and for storage of Temple vessels and instruments.

Three Principal Supports

As Masons we are taught that a Lodge has three principal

supports or pillars, denominated Wisdom, Strength and Beauty. The pillar of Wisdom (to contrive) on the right, the pillar of Strength (to support) on the left, and the pillar of Beauty (to adorn) in the center.

Three Steps, The

usually delineated upon the Master's carpet, are emblematical of the three principal stages of human life, viz.: Youth, Manhood, and Age. In Youth, as Entered Apprentices, we ought industriously to occupy our minds in the attainments of useful knowledge; in Manhood, as Fellow Crafts, we should apply our knowledge to the discharge of our respective duties to God, our neighbor, and ourselves; that so, in Age, as Master Masons, we may enjoy the happy reflection consequent on a well-spent life, and die in the hope of a glorious immortality.

Tiler (Tyler)

In operative Masonry, the workman known as the Tiler placed over the finished edifice a roof of tiles, and thus provided protection for the building. The symbolism of his work is invested in the office of Tiler (spelled Tyler in some jurisdictions) in speculative Masonry. His duty is to provide protection for the Lodge when it is organized and ready for business, closing the doors, keeping away eavesdroppers and intruders, and guarding the sacred precincts from intrusions of any kind.

Token

This is from the Greek *deigma*, meaning example, or proof — the origin of the word "teach," and in its orginal sense had much the same meaning as sign and symbol, for it was an object used as the sign of something else. It is generally used, however, in the sense of a pledge or of an object that proves something. In our usage a token is something that exhibits, or shows, or proves that we are Masons — the grip of recognition, for example.

Tongue of Good Report

having a good reputation; those who know you report that you are a good man; a credit to yourself and to society.

Troubles of Life

Freemasonry recognizes the fact that man in his sin-fallen state is the natural heir to sufferings, frailties, weaknesses, trial and troubles; and that release and renewal of strength may be found only in God and the use of the means of Divine Grace and Providence.

Trowel, The

is an instrument made use of by operative Masons to spread the cement which unites the building into one common mass; but we, as Free and Accepted Masons, are taught to make use of it for the  more noble and glorious purpose of spreading the cement of brotherly love and affection; that cement which unites us into one sacred band or society of friends and brothers, among whom no contention should ever exist, but that noble contention, or rather emulation, of who best can work and best agree.

Trust in God

In this life, mans knows not what an hour or a day may bring forth. Paths upon which he must travel are unknown, and many unseen and unexpected dangers await him. Even when among friends, there is a constant need for Divine wisdom, sustenance, strength, aid and guidance. Hence, as the candidate crosses the threshold of the Lodge, and throughout all the ceremonies and rites of Freemasonry, he is required to "put his trust in God."

Truth

Truth is a divine attribute and the foundation of every virtue. To be good and true is the first lesson we are taught in Masonry. On this theme we contemplate, and by its dictates endeavor to regulate our conduct. Hence, while influenced by this principle, hypocrisy and deceit are unknown among us; sincerity and plain dealing distinguish us; and with heart and tongue we join in promoting each other's welfare and rejoicing in each other's prosperity.

Tubal-cain

The son of Lamech, a descendant of Adam through the Cainite line, Tubal-cain is regarded in Masonry as the father of skilled workmanship in artistic productions for building purposes.

Tuscan

one of the five orders of architecture, originated in the Tuscany area of southern Italy.

Twenty-Four Inch Gauge

is an instrument made use of by operative Masons to measure and lay out their work. But we, as Free and Accepted Masons, are taught to make use of it for the more noble and glorious  purpose of dividing our time. It, being divided into twenty-four equal parts, is emblematic of the twenty-four hours of the day, which we are taught to divide into three parts, whereby we find a part for the service of God and a distressed worthy brother; a part for our usual vocations; and a part for refreshment and repose.

U

Unity

The mystic tie of true fraternalism is love. But, even where brotherly love prevails, differences of opinion, conflicting ideas, unenlightenment on the part of some, prejudices and varied interests in life endanger the spirit of genuine fellowship and unity. Hence, Masons are constantly taught to avoid "confusion among the workmen," discord, strife, jealousies and vain discussions on non-essentials; and to cultivate zealously and fervently the spirit of true unity in the Lodge and in the Fraternity.

Undiscovered Country From Whose Bourne No Traveler Returns

that which lies beyond death; the afterlife (Shakespeare, *Hamlet*: Act III, Scene 1)

Usual Vocation

your job or profession; the manner in which you make your living.

Untempered Mortar

The use of mortar not composed of the correct ingredients or in which these ingredients are improperly mixed in operative Masonry is certain to result in a weak and defective building, in a building that will soon disintegrate and tumble down. In speculative Masonry, such untempered mortar is symbolic of dishonest and fraudulent mixtures in the building of character or in the construction of the institution of Freemasonry. It represents hypocrisy, the representation of evil as good, the employment of bad materials in moral, ethical and spiritual architecture.

V

Veiled Allegory

Uttering a thing in parabolic form (i.e., parable) with its meaning hidden. Many of the sublimest truths of Freemasonry are thus spoken, and even those who have been given the mysteries of speculative science must delve into the caverns of Masonic mystery to gather these hidden gems of truth.

Veil of the Temple

This was the curtain or partition which separated the Holy Place from the Most Holy Place. It served as a constant reminder to worshippers than only the High Priest, and he only once a year after having made proper atonement for his own sins and for the sins of the people, was allowed to enter the Holy of Holies. As a result of the atonement of Christ in his death on the cross, this veil was rent and destroyed, and through Him as High Priest an open door into the Heavenly Sanctuary has been prepared for all true worshippers.

Vicissitudes

the successive, alternating or changing phases or conditions of life or fortune; ups and downs; the difficulties of life; difficulties or hardships which are part of a way of life or career

Vide Aude Tace

Latin for: *See, Dare, Be Silent*

Vide Audi Tace

Latin for: *See, Hear, Be Silent*

Virtus Junkxit Mors Non Separabit

Latin for: *Whom Virtue Unites, Death will not separate*

Visitors

The laws of ancient Israel with respect to the treatment of strangers or visitors have full recognition and force among Freemasons. In fact, no Mason is allowed to regard as a stranger or visitor any Brother Mason, even though he has no acquaintance with him, and even if he may be of some other religion, country or nationality.

Vouch

to give personal assurances; give a guarantee. This harks back to the Latin *vocare*, to call, to summon, and is the origin of voice, vouchsafe, vocation (in the sense of a "calling"), vocal, etc. To vouch is to raise one's voice in testimony, to bear witness, to affirm, to call to witness. If we vouch for a brother we raise the voice to testify that we know him to be a regular Mason.

Vouchsafe

to condescend to grant or bestow (a privilege, for example); deign.

Vows

The "vows of a Mason" are the inward and spiritual covenants of the mystic ties of the Fraternity which have their outward expression in the formal obligations assumed in the several Degrees of the Order. The vows are the covenants of heart and conscience which serve as the main force of heart and character in faithfully observing the obligations verbally expressed before the altar.

W

Wages

Wage, of which wages is the collective plural, remotely descended from the Latin *vas*, having the meaning of pledge, security, pawn, or a promise to pay backed up by security. After it entered into modern languages it had a peculiar history; it became *gage*, a pledge or pawn, appearing

in our engage, disengage, etc., but having no relation with gage, one of our Working Tools; "wager" in the sense of a bet; in another context it became "wed," the act of marrying, so called because of the pledges given; and "wage" in the sense of compensation for service given. An "allowance" is a one-sided form of payment, depending on the will of the giver; a "stipend" is a fixed sum, usually nominal, and is supposed to be paid as per a permanent arrangement; a "salary" (from *sal*, or salt, the old pay given soldiers) is an amount fixed by contract, and estimated over a relatively long period of time, year or month; "wages" are paid to laborers over short periods of time, or at the completion of the required task. It is certain that the operative Masons who labored in the construction of King Solomon's Temple were paid wages, but there is no Biblical reference as to the daily wage paid. In Speculative Masonry the Master Mason symbolically receives "wages," rather than salary, because they represent the rewards that come to him as rapidly as he does his work; and, as the etymology of the word suggests, they are certain, something one may bank on.

Warden

"Ward" is of Medieval origin, having been used in early English, French, German, etc., always in the sense of to guard something, a meaning preserved in warden, guard, guardian, wary, ware, ward, etc. A warden is guardian of the west gate of the Temple, the Junior Warden of the south gate.

Warrant

This also derives from the same source, and carries the general meaning of "to defend," "to guard." Warrant is sometimes used as a pledge of security; in Masonry it is a document officially issued to authorize the formation of a Lodge, and consequently acts as the pledge, or security, for the future activity of it.

Wayfaring Man

A traveler or transient, one with no settled home, is often referred to as a wayfaring man.

White

White is symbolic of purity in its various uses in Masonry.

White Stone

The white stone is a token of fraternal friendship and helpfulness as well as enduring alliance.

Widow's Son

Masons are sometimes referred to as "sons of the widow" as this was the title applied to Hiram, chief architect of Solomon's Temple.

Widows and Orphans

Masons are solemnly pledged to make special provision for widows and orphans in need, especially among families of the Fraternity.

Winding Stairs

The Temple of Solomon was equipped with an impressive winding stairway consisting of fifteen steps leading from the porch to the second floor. Elaborate and extensive symbolisms are attached to these winding stairs in the work of Freemasonry.

Wisdom of Solomon

In ancient Craft Masonry, King Solomon stands as the representative of the highest degree of wisdom. The East, the source of light, symbolizes for every true Mason the wisdom needed for success in life. The East is represented by the pillar that supports the Lodge and by the Worshipful Master.

Word

In all of its several and varied uses, the term WORD symbolizes Divine Truth. The search for the Word in any sense means ultimately the search for Truth. The whole system of speculative Masonry is, in its essence, the search for Truth. The written word of God hold a pre-eminent place in all Degrees of Masonry and in all of its teachings.

Worshipful

As used in Worshipful Master, from the Anglo-Saxon, worthship (worthy); honorable or respectable. Used as a respectful form of address. The term has no religious or sacred implication.

Y

Yod

A Hebrew letter equivalent in sound to I or Y. It is the initial letter of the word Jehovah, the Tetragrammaton, and hence was peculiarly sacred among the Talmudists. In Symbolic Freemasonry, the yod has been replaced by the letter G. But in the advanced Degrees it is retained, and within a triangle, as in the illustration, constitutes the symbol of the Deity.

York Rite

A system of Masonry termed by Albert Mackey (when worked in the U.S.) the *American Rite*. In the U.S., the York Rite begins in the craft lodge and continues to the degree of Knight Templar. Only a handful of lodges in the U.S. work any ritual other than the Webb based York Rite ritual.

Z

Zabulon

The Greek wording of Zebulun, the tenth son of Jacob. In the Royal Arch Zabulon represents one of the stones in the Pectoral or Breastplate.

Zaphnath-Paaneah

An Egyptian title given to the Patriarch Joseph by the Egyptian King under whom he was Viceroy. The name has been interpreted Revealer of secrets, and is a password in the old instructions of the Ancient and Accepted Scottish Rite.

Zeal

enthusiasm; diligence; eagerness and great interest in pursuit of something.

Zenith

That point in the heavens which is vertical to the spectator, and from which a perpendicular line passing through him and extended would reach the center of the earth. From of old the documents of the Ancient and Accepted Scottish Rite are dated "under the Celestial Canopy of the Zenith which answers to --- "; the latitude of the place whence the document is issued being then given to fill the blank space. The latitude alone is expressed because that indicates the position of the sun's meridian height. Longitude, however, is always omitted, because every place whence such a document is issued is called the Grand East, the specific spot where the sun rises. The theory implied is, that although the South of the Lodge may vary, its chief point must always be in the East, the point of the sun rising, where longitude begins.

Zion

Mount Zion was the southwestern of the three hills which constituted the high table-land on which Jerusalem was built. It was the royal residence and hence it is often called the City of David. The name is sometimes used as synonymous with Jerusalem.

More Books from Cornerstone

Robert's Rules of Order: Masonic Edition
Revised by Michael R. Poll
Softcover $17.95
ISBN 1-887560-07-6

Our Stations and Places
Masonic Officer's Handbook
Revised by Michael R. Poll
Softcover $16.95
ISBN 1-887560-63-7

Masonic Questions and Answers
by Paul M. Bessel
Softcover $16.95
ISBN 1-887560-59-9

Knights & Freemasons: The Birth of Modern Freemasonry
By Albert Pike & Albert Mackey
Edited by Michael R. Poll
Foreword by S. Brent Morris
Softcover $16.95
ISBN 1-887560-66-1

A.E. Waite: Words From a Masonic Mystic
Edited by Michael R. Poll
Foreword by Joseph Fort Newton
Softcover $16.95
ISBN 1-887560-73-4

Dragonflies - Journeys into the Paranormal
by Evelyn Klebert
Softcover $12.95
ISBN 1-887560-72-6

Cornerstone Book Publishers
www.cornerstonepublishers.com

More Books from Cornerstone

Masonic Enlightenment
The Philosophy, History and Wisdom of Freemasonry
Edited by Michael R. Poll
Softcover $18.95
ISBN 1-887560-75-0

Éliphas Lévi and the Kabbalah
by Robert L. Uzzel
Softcover $18.95
ISBN 1-887560-76-9

Off in a Dream
A collection of poetry and prose
by Aubrey Damhnait Fae
Softcover $14.95
ISBN 1-887560-72-6

A Ghost of a Chance
by Evelyn Klebert
Softcover $12.95
ISBN 1-887560-50-5

In the Twinkling of a Star
Collected and arranged by
Sis. Joyce Fuller, OES PHA
Softcover $15.00
ISBN 1-887560-77-7

Freemasons and Rosicrucians - the Enlightened
by Manly P. Hall
Edited by Michael R. Poll
Softcover $16.95
ISBN 1-887560-58-0

Cornerstone Book Publishers
www.cornerstonepublishers.com

Breinigsville, PA USA
31 May 2010
238975BV00001B/5/A